Indian Marriage

Customs and Rituals

Indian Marriage

Customs and Rituals

R N Kogata • Lalita Kogata

D.K. Printworld (P) Ltd.
New Delhi

Cataloging in Publication Data — DK
[Courtesy: D.K. Agencies (P) Ltd. <docinfo@dkagencies.com>]

Kogata, R. N. (Ram Narayan), 1964–
Indian marriage : customs and rituals / R.N. Kogata, Lalita Kogata.
p. cm.
Includes verses in Sanskrit (Devanagari and roman); with English translation.
ISBN 13: 9788124604939
ISBN 10: 8124604932

1. Marriage customs and rites, Hindu — India. 2. Marriage in art. 3. Gaṇeśa (Hindu deity) — Art. 4. Art, Hindu. I. Kogata, Lalita, 1965–, joint author. II. Title.

DDC 294.538 095 4 22

First published in Hindi, 2006
English translation first published in 2009
ISBN 13: 978-81-246-0493-9
ISBN 10: 81-246-0493-2

Translation arranged by D.K. Printworld (P) Ltd., New Delhi

A Creation of:
Mr. R.N. Kogata
Mrs. Lalita Kogata
608, Hiran Magari, Sector-11, Udaipur - India
Phone : +91-94141-58870
devkush@rediffmail.com

Published and printed by:
D.K. Printworld (P) Ltd.
'Sri Kunj' F-52, Bali Nagar
Ramesh Nagar Metro Stn., New Delhi - 110 015
Phs.: 011-2545 3975, 2546 6019
Fax: 011-2546 5926
Email: dkprintworld@vsnl.net
Web: www.dkprintworld.com

मातु उमा सुत गजवदन, पावन सुन्दर वेश ।
बन्दहुँ प्रथम गजाननम् , गौरी पुत्र गणेश ।।
विघ्नहरण मंगलकरण, गणनायक सर्वेश ।
ध्यावहुँ प्रथम गजाननम् , प्रियसुत उमा महेश ।।
गौरी पुत्रो गणाध्यक्षो विघ्नहर्ता विनायकः ।
वैवाहिक विध्वत्र मंगल विदधातुनः ।।

maatu umaa suta gajavadana, paavana sundara vesha ।
bandhahoom prathama gajaananam, gauri putra ganesha ।।
vighnaharana, mangalakarana, gananaayaka sarvesha ।
dhyaavahoom prathama gajaananam, priyasuta umaa mahesha ।।
gauri putro ganaadhyaksho, vighnahartaa vinaayakah ।
vaivaahika vidhvatra mangala vidadhaatunah ।।

हे गौरी पुत्र ! हे गणाध्यक्ष ! हे विघ्नहर्ता ! हे मंगलकर्ता ! हे गणनायक ! हे विनायक ! हम आपका सर्वप्रथम ध्यान करके आपसे प्रार्थना करते हैं कि आप हमारे वैवाहिक विधि-विधानों को मंगलमय करने हेतु हमारे यहां विराजमान हों ।

O Son of Gauri ! O Chief of hosts ! O Remover of obstacles ! O Bestower of auspiciousness ! O Lord of hosts ! O one without a lord !
First of all we invoke you and pray to you that you be gracious enough to be present here to bless the rites, rituals and ceremonies we conduct during this marriage function with auspiciousness and success ! Our salutations to you again !!

प्रेयो मित्रं बन्धुता वा समग्रा
सर्वे कामाः शेवधिर्जीवितं वा ।
स्त्रीणां भर्ता धर्मदाराश्च पुंसा-
मित्यन्योन्यं वत्सयोर्ज्ञातमस्तु ॥

— भवभूति

पत्नियों के लिये पति
और पतियों के लिये उनकी पत्नी
है संसार की प्रियतम जन ।

और है सर्वश्रेष्ठ मित्र
आधारशिला सम्पूर्ण पारिवारिक सम्बन्धों की
पूर्तिदायक समस्त कामनाओं की
अक्षय निधि सम्पूर्ण सुखों की ।

हैं एक-दूसरे के प्राणस्वरूप वो
है विवाह का मर्म जो ।

— भवभूति

The Husband and Wife
Most adored objects of life!

Best companion to each other
ideal, familial and together
Fulfilment of life desires!

Immense treasure of values and feelings
Makes life most cheering!

The true marital life core
Experience and go far!

— Bhavabhuti

Preface

First we invoke the Lord of the Gods, the chief of the hosts, the omnipresent guide and helpmate, Lord Vinayakji, to assist us in conducting the ceremonies, according to our culture.

In return for his beneficient leelaas and assistance our culture reveres and respects Vinayakji as the first God to be worshipped with devotion before we start any work.

We are ever grateful that Bhagwan Ganesh has chosen us through his Grace to undertake the writing of this book. At every moment of our life we have experienced the magnificence of his Grace and it is our firm belief that whatever be the act or deed, nothing happens without the blessing of Sri Ganapati. "Ganapati is everywhere, Ganapati is in everyone's mind, the whole universe came out of Ganapati," this is our conviction which has been supported by the various Puranas and literature. We have tried to see Ganapati in different forms, colours, in every creature, every deed, all the time, while standing, sitting, sleeping and while wide-awake, and by his Grace we have succeeded. Through various incidents, happenings and associations we have realised the connections of Ganapati's picture or idol with our lives and have etched his figure in our minds.

In order to create spiritual awareness and to rid the humanity of impurities, our ancient rishis and munis have formulated some doctrines and rules by following which we can purify the soul of a child, at the time of its conception, from its sins accumulated from all its previous births and imbibe it with noble thoughts. The idea behind these doctrines is that a man can lead his present life with noble purpose and unblemished culture. Good sacraments give in one's life, happiness, merriment, plenitude, progress, addition of virtues, an assured place in heaven after death and a re-birth in a noble family. Therefore, it is essential for the present and future generations to have a thorough knowledge of our well-intentioned sacraments.

After following the various sacraments, one day the idea came to our mind that we should associate Ganapati with the rituals connected with the popular customs of marriage in our society, and see Ganapati taking part in all the ceremonies. The result is that we have narrated here, in brief, sixteen important sacraments, together with detailed description of the various ceremonies involved in the sacraments and the different items required for the proper conduct of the ceremonies, so that we can bring out a book, which is both authentic and authoritative. These sacraments have scientific and social importance, but we have refraimed from making any comment on them or interpreting them to prove or justify their rightness. The days now are not for joint families; people do not have the time to conduct ceremonies as required by custom; and, to add to these, there is no detailed or complete information about the ceremonies. Further, we tend to follow Western culture blindly to such an extent that we may even forget our own Indian or Hindu culture. An effort has been made to give as much detailed information as possible on the different sacraments so that we can not only preserve our valued heritage and culture intact, but also enjoy the ceremonies in the company of our families.

People have different opinions about the marriage of Lord Ganesh. Some say that Ganeshji is not married at all. But in Brahmavaivarta Purana, Shiva Purana, Ganesha Purana, Mudgal Purana, Narad Purana, etc. there are descriptions about Ganeshji's wedding and about his marrying Riddhi and Siddhi. After going through all those writings we decided to portray Ganeshji as the bridegroom in this book. We have done this with a clear mind, pure heart and unflinching faith or bhakti in Bhagawan Ganapati. But, knowingly or unknowingly, if we have wounded anyone's sentiments, we seek pardon from those affected and from Bhagawan Sri Ganesh.

We are indeed delighted and grateful to His Highness Shriji Arvind Singh Mewar for his worthy guidance and support from time to time, without which our dream would not have come true. For collection of material for the book, we have taken the help of not only our elders, vidwans, pandits and purohits but also various scriptures and books on the subject — we are grateful to all of them. We cannot, and we will not, forget the blessings of our parents Shri Bhairav Lal Kogata and Smt Kanchan Devi Kogata and Prof K.M. Nuwal and Smt Kamla Devi Nuwal due to which we have always got success after success and reached to this status in our life.

We crave the love and blessings of everyone.

R.N. Kogata
Lalita Kogata

Contents

The Sixteen Rituals and Sacraments as described by Maharishi Ved Vyas in Vyas-Smriti

|| Sri Ganeshaaya Namah ||

Only the intelligent persons can make the best use of the physical resources available on this planet. On the other hand, if these resources are given to foolish and dull-headed persons, it will only result in chaos, misery and destruction all around. Man's superiority does not lie in accessing these natural resources, but in how best he can make use of them to achieve his goal.

It is the supreme spirit which has been responsible for man's superiority over other beings and the growth of his inner self. The materialists who were only physical thinkers, desired for the growth of material resources only. This led to the decline of the human self and gave impetus to the growth of physical resources all around. The consequences are before us today. In spite of having gained access to all the natural resources, man feels he is yet incomplete, unhappy and unsatisfied. In his aim for grabbing more wealth, he has strayed away from understanding his own supreme self. He is living a false life enwrapped in the glare of this physical world. Human character is on the decline and we can say that this is all due to the curse of physical materialism growing rapidly the world over.

All religions of the world have emphasized on the supreme human being and his growth so that a true human character develops. The fundamental aim of our Indian tradition was to develop a whole man, a great personality, the one who believed his supreme self. Our sages had aimed for the growth of spiritual knowledge in preference to the physical development.

The Indian sages always preached to us to rise above parochialism and casteism and to always think about the welfare of humanity as a whole. They emphasized that man is the only one highly developed, both physically and mentally amongst all beings, on this planet but he is the only being that is going against the law of nature, slowly digging his own grave and suffering the maximum.

There are three basic principles in every human life. First is his **self-awareness** or *aatmaa* which gives him life. This dwells in the body and is known as *aatmaa* or soul. This *aatmaa* is only a part of the *paramaatmaa* or Almighty, who is omnipresent, and though it is not separated from the latter, yet due to its association with the human mind, intellect, knowledge and egoism it maintains a distance and is referred to as "the individual soul" or *jeevaatmaa* the power of "self-awareness." When the individual soul attains complete self-awareness it gets merged into the *Brahman*, the all-powerful — the Almighty.

Mind is the second basic principle of human life. It is the important creation of this "self-awareness" which ultimately becomes the cause of our deeds and our destiny. Therefore, the ultimate cause of our deeds is not our "soul power" but our "mind power." When a particular work is done repeatedly, it becomes a practice. This practice forms a thick layer deep inside the heart and soul and after the death of the physical body the layer remains there in the subtle body. When the soul enters into a new body, it causes the fresh body (in which it has entered) to perform similar functions. These are called our "deeds" or *karma*. These deeds go on accumulating with every new birth and form a huge storehouse, which is called "collective deeds." Only a small part of these "collective deeds" is used up in the whole of one's lifespan in which he is prompted to perform his day-to-day tasks.

At the time of death, only the physical body perishes, while the subtle body remains attached with the soul for generations. It is this subtle body that acts as a carrier of the good or bad deeds. These mixed deeds enter a body at the time of a new baby's birth along with the deeds of parents and thus help in forming the character of that new being entering this world. They also have an effect even when it is in the womb.

A man performs several inauspicious deeds due to selfish interests, sexual needs, foolishness, greed, infatuation, ego satisfaction, desire fulfilment, spot reaction, anger, hypocrisy, etc. These acts of his turn into thoughts and lie deep inside his mind. These thoughts induce the person to perform several duties and mould his character in his new life. These thoughts or instincts not only make a man do certain types of work but they also do not allow him to do some other types of work. Today, we can change our bad deeds of the past into good deeds or *karma*s and even alter them with the help of virtuous knowledge, by following the teachings of *guru*s and saints, by attaining good education, having a healthy environment around, etc. This is the work of *purushaartha*. The deeds or *karma*s of our past rise and influence our present life, and they are called *praarabdha karma*s. *Purushaartha* denotes the deeds or *karma*s that are being done in the present life, and this is stronger than *praarabdha* because it can change the bad *karma*s of one's past lives into good *karma*s. It is the lack of proper knowledge which keeps a man bound to his past deeds.

Every work performed has an end-result. No action is complete if it does not end in a result. It is mentioned in our scriptures, अवश्यमेव भोक्तव्यम् कृतं कर्म शुभाशुभम् (*avashyameva bhoktavyam kritam karma shubhaashubham*), means a man has to certainly experience the results of all good or bad deeds performed by him. Though the results are definite the ways of performing the work can be changed and new good deeds done to reduce the effect of any new bad deeds.

The third basic principle of man is his **body** which helps him in concluding all the tasks undertaken by him. "Mind" is the cause for all actions but all actions are done with the help of the body. In devotion to God, "body" plays a vital role. Without it no task can be completed. Therefore body should not be neglected at all. It is the combination of both body and mind that develops the soul.

As there are three principles in life, similarly there are three basics for any deed or *karma* to be completed. The first and the important basic requirement is the **power of knowledge** or *jnaan shakti.* It is with this power of knowledge that one performs all the work diligently and satisfactorily. If the knowledge is lacking, the work will remain incomplete. Therefore, only knowledge is basic for development and success in one's life. The second basic need is the **power of wealth** or *dhan shakti* and the third is the **power of body** or *shaareerik shakti*. With the passage of time, the mind of a person develops and there is a possibility of mind misusing these three powers — knowledge, wealth and body. But it is the "knowledge" which reaches the strong-willed person and makes him do good things for others. Therefore, it is essential that mind should be cleansed and kept pure.

All the religions of the world endeavour to make man a Supreme Being. They simply give advices like "do this," "do not do this," etc. But this has not brought much improvement in man. He has been repeatedly told about the future good life in Heaven and suffering in Hell, but this has not reduced his bad demeanour or deeds. By only dusting the leaves of trees, one cannot expect to have sweet fruits. For this, one has to sow good seeds. If the seed is defective, then expecting tasty fruits from the tree is only futile and not possible. Material prosperity cannot make a man great, nor can bodily development improve him. Today, the material resources have developed to the maximum, but humanism or humanness is steadily on the decline. It is this material nature which could be the cause of destruction of life on this planet earth, unless those who utilize these natural resources become honest, cultured, and well-intentioned, well-wishers of the universe. Greatness of man cannot be measured by his wealth or material prosperity, but only by his good behaviour, conduct, honesty, truthfulness, and sincerity.

In the first instance, from where and why all these unwanted evils entered a man's mind are some of the questions which worried Indian thinkers. Indian scholars pondered over these questions and have come to the conclusion that lack of culture was the main cause.

To eradicate all the evils from human mind Indian thinkers adopted several ways by which a man could have good thoughts, speak good words, do good deeds and become cultured. One of the ways mentioned in our Vedic scriptures is observance of various rituals and ceremonies. Good and bad deeds of the past lives create good and bad thoughts resulting in a man doing good and bad deeds in his present life. A man is born as a result of, and with, the *karma*s of his previous birth/s, and they influence his day-to-day life and nature. The bad deeds or *karma*s can be transformed into good *karma* by the rites and rituals prescribed by the scriptures, which cover his whole life right from his birth till his death, i.e. from the cradle to the grave.

Sages in India inform us that pleasure does not lie in material objects. Pleasure is only a mental state to obtain which a healthy mind is a must. If a person, in spite of attaining everything, remains discontented and unhappy, his mind is always disturbed by physical and mental tensions.

Spiritualists in India lay stress on man's superiority, the great society in which he lives and the high principles he follows. He considers the material objects as just means to achieve a goal and not the means in itself. The spiritual man does not want to weaken a person by asking him to shun all the material objects and pleasures but he talks of a strong and superior person who could be a blessing for the society and not a liability to it. Keeping the mind healthy is the only way to achieve this goal. For the sake of purifying the mind, the Hindu religion prescribes sixteen ceremonies, which cover the whole life cycle of man — from his birth till his death.

To prove the superiority of man, it is essential that all his physical and mental faculties are revived. It is no use giving sermons to him or preaching the divine words to him. For this all the sixteen sacraments, from birth till death, have to be observed religiously, and only then can one expect some good results. To revive these sacraments and work for the welfare of mankind, India has adopted this religious path which works for purifying the heart and soul.

There are three superior powers in this world — knowledge, wealth and energy. Most of the tasks in this world depend on these three powers only and without their help no task can be accomplished. It is our inner consciousness, the mind, which allows us to use or misuse the resources.

The power may be of various kinds. To use it or misuse it totally depends on one's own mentality. To change one's mentality and mind, these rituals or ceremonies have been introduced in our life. They can change all the bad deeds of our past lives into good *karma* and make our present life beautiful and worth living.

Man's life is not the result of any union, nor an accidental happening but it is created by nature with a clear purpose. The aim of life is not to simply live our lives till we die, or to enjoy the pleasures available, but to constantly develop our self-consciousness and to attain liberation or *moksha* in the end. The only way to develop our self-consciousness is by destroying our bad qualities and having in their place good qualities and virtues. By doing this, man gets happiness, peace and prosperity in this life and attains a glorious state in the after-life as well. Our ancient sages have prescribed certain rituals following which one can protect one's caste identity and honour, do his duties diligently, develop his consciousness and achieve the ultimate goal of his life.

It is clearly mentioned in our scriptures that on completion of the rituals, one becomes a twice-born — संस्कारात् द्विज उच्येत (*samskaaraat dvij uchyate*). The word *dvij* means a second birth. The first birth, given by our parents, happens due to the unspent accumulation of good and bad deeds or *karma* from our previous births. The bad qualities of the past are removed and replaced by good virues, and by this man get a new life or birth which is better than the previous natural birth. The new life makes a man decent, cultured, service-minded and selfless.

It is also said : जन्मना जायेत शूद्रः (*janmanaa jaayate shudrah*), i.e. we all are *shudras* by birth. Here the word *shudra* does not refer to person of the fourth caste or *varna* but it means a person who is not mentally or physically developed, whose knowledge is very poor, who is worried only about his own self and his food, who is devoid of education and culture, in whom the basic faculties have not developed, who lacks in grasping the truth and who does not think about his society. Such a crude person is called a *shudra.* All these qualities are not developed in a child, and therefore a child is called a *shudra.* Later, this child gets proper education, moves in a decent society and atmosphere and his mental faculties develop to make him a proper and refined human being. He is being developed so that he can imbibe the good virtues in life and he is taught the proper art of living. These ceremonies and rituals help in changing and directing his mind on the way to progress and prosperity.

The system by which a person's past faults and misdeeds are transformed into virtues is called purification or *samskaar.* The medium through which this purification is done is called a purificatory rite or ceremony. It is similar to purifying gold by melting it in fire. In the same way medicine is purified by removing all the impurities, and a washerman washes and removes the dirt and stains from clothes to make them look new. A farmer experiments with seeds, uses various irrigation methods, changes fertilizers and pesticides so that he gets better quality and quantity of yield from his fields. In the same way, to beget the best progeny, a man is required to develop his physical, mental and intellectual faculties and keep them healthy.

Without observence of these rituals and sacraments a person will only remain confined to himself under pressure from his past deeds and can never progress. Actions are the result of his thoughts only. It is the thinking which guides him to act and perform a certain task. Therefore, he has to keep his mind healthy and pure so that healthy and pure actions are taken throughout his life — from impregnation till death.

The main aim of these ceremonies is to remove the evils of the past misdeeds, and inspire one to do virtuous deeds.

संस्करणं गुणान्तराधानं संस्कारः (*samskaranam gunaantaraadhaanam samskaarah*), meaning, remove all bad thoughts from your mind, purify your thoughts, imbibe good qualities and virtues and make your mind full of good qualities.

According to *Gautam Dharmasutra*, by purification ceremonies our misdeeds are destroyed and are replaced by good qualities.

According to Shankaracharya,

> संस्कारो हि नाम संस्कार्यस्य
> गुणाधानेन वा स्याद्योषापनयनेन वा ।
> — ब्रह्मसूत्र भाष्य 1.1.4
>
> *samskaaro hi naama samskaaryasy*
> *gunaadhaanena vaa syaadyoshaapanayanen vaa*
> — *Brahmasutra Bhaashya* 1.1.4
>
> *meaning*, inducing virtuous thoughts in person's mind and removing the past evils from it is called purification or *samskaar.* According to Maharishi Charaka,
>
> संस्कारो हि गुणान्तराधानमुच्यते
>
> *saṁskaaro hi gunaantaraadhaanamuchyate*
>
> *meaning* depositing of good qualities in a person or product is called purification.

It is also written in *Samskaar Vidhi*,

> जन्मना जायते शूद्रऽसंस्काराद्द्विज उच्यते
>
> *janmanaa jaayate shudra 'samskaaraaddvija uchyate*
>
> *meaning*, by birth all are *shudras* (crude persons) and the good qualities purify a person and give him a second birth.

Our sages and saints believed that passions and accumulated over several births leave their impression in the soul or *aatmaa*. The soul enters a new body and strives to do deeds and satisfy the desires. In this process a person accumulates more desires, and in this way he remains a slave to his instincts for ever.

According to followers of Mimamsa philosophy कर्म बीजं संस्कारः (*karmbeejam samskaarah*), meaning, our instincts are the seeds of our actions, and तन्निमित्ता सृष्टि (*tatrimittaa srishti*), meaning, that is the main reason for creation of life.

Each person's behaviour is influenced not only by his past deeds or *karma* but also by his present surroundings — his family, his relatives and his friends. To preserve the purity and honour of his caste, a person has to follow certain rites which are very imporant in his life. The reasons for one's misdeeds are many — the society, environment, education, physical and mental problems, etc. These result in defective progenies with bad or evil characteristics. The evil characteristics are changed into virtues by the purificatory rites which have great significance in preserving virtues in a society for the present as well as future generations.

These rituals have influenced man in unique ways. At the time of performing ceremonies various ritual acts, *yagya*s, *mantra* recitation, etc. are done, which have been scientifically proved beneficial through sound principles, magnetic power transmission, light and colour effect, etc. Most importantly, they fill the mind with noble and virtuous thoughts. An alert and pure mind is the best servant and guide to a soul, in leading a life of honour in this world.

During the performance of various ceremonies through *purohit*s we can feel the divine presence when we invite and receive the various gods; we can feel the pure and serene atmosphere when we do *yagya*s or sacrifices; we feel happy in the presence of our relatives and friends; and we have the mental satifaction of having done our duty according to the scriptures.

Different scholars have mentioned different numbers of rituals and sacraments. In *Gautam-Smriti*, there is a list of 40 ceremonies — चत्वारिंशत्संस्कारैः संस्कृतः (*catvaarimshatsamskaaraih samskritah*). Somewhere we find 48 rituals, while Maharishi Angiras has mentioned 25 sacraments. According to the followers of *Dasa Karma Paddhati* there are ten ceremonies. But Maharishi Veda Vyasa in his *Vyasa-Smriti* has described sixteen rituals as important.

गर्भाधानं पुंसवनं सीमांतो जातकर्म च ।
नामक्रियानिष्क्रमणेऽन्नशनं वपन क्रिया ॥
कर्णवेधो व्रतादेशो वेदारम्भक्रियाविधिः ।
केशांतः स्नानमुद्वाहो विवाहाग्निपरिग्रहः ॥
त्रेताग्निसंग्रहश्चेति संस्काराः षोडश स्मृताः ।
— व्याससस्मृति 1/13-15

garbhaadhaanam pumsavanam
seemaanto jaatakarma cha ।
naamakriyaanishkramane
'nnashanam vapana kriyaa ॥
karnavedho vrataadesho
vedaarambha kriyaavidhih ।
keshaantah snaanamudvaaho
vivaahaagni parigrahah ॥
tretaagni samgrahashceti
samskaaraah shodasha smritah ।
— *Vyasa-Smriti* 1/13-15

The *karma* section of the Vedas approves of only 16 sacraments as discussed in detail below. The first eight rituals deal with worldly pursuits and the remaining eight help in the spiritual path. Undoubtedly, ceremonies which are performed ritualistically on assigned days and time periods can bestow extraordinary benefits.

1. Garbhaadaan Samskaar

The most important goal of married life is to be blessed with a progeny with excellent qualities, and which is healthy, meritorious, prosperous and cultured. To get the best children the couple has to sexually unite at an auspicious moment by observing a ceremony called *garbhaadhaan* or "ritual impregnation." For this ceremony the father and mother should prepare themselves physically and mentally as the offspring to be born will be an image of themselves.

Smrti Samgraha mentions about *garbhaadhaan* as:

निषेकाद् बैजिकं चैनो गार्भिकं चापमृज्यते ।
क्षेत्रसंस्कारसिद्धिश्च गर्भाधानफलं स्मृतम् ॥

nishekaad baijikam chaino
gaarbhikam chaapamrijyate ।
kshetrasamskaarasidhishcha
garbhaadhaanaphalam smritam ॥

meaning, with proper rites and rituals, a good and worthy progeny is attained through *garbhaadhaan*. This ritual helps in destroying the sins related to sperm count or pregnancy and the evil effects on the child to be born, if any.

Sushruta Samhitaa mentions about *garbhaadhaan* thus:

आहाराचारचेष्टाभिर्यादृशोभिः समन्वितौ ।
स्त्रीपुंसौ समुपेयातां तयोः पुत्रोऽपि तादृशः ॥
— सुश्रुत संहिता/शारीर/2.46.50

aahaaraacaaraceshta
abhiryaadrishobhih samanvitau ।
streepumsau samupeyaataam
tayoh putro'pi taadrishah ॥
— *Sushruta Samhita/Shaareera*/2.46.50

For healthy and proper coitus to take place, besides proper diet, it is essential that the characters and efforts of both husband and wife unite simultaneously. The son born through this union reflects their character only.

God Dhanvantari says, after *ritusnaan* in whichever way a woman sees her husband, likewise a son is born. This means, if a woman wishes to beget a son with her husband's ideal characterstics, or one who is as brave as Abhimanyu, as devout as Dhruva, as spiritual as King Janaka, and as generous as Karna, she should bathe on the fourth day after menstruation and become chaste, pay obeisance to her elders and *gurus*, and unite with her husband in the night at the auspicious time. If impregnation takes place during the third phase of night, i.e. between 12.00 midnight and 3.00 a.m. the son to be born will be a devotee of God and a follower of righteousness.

Keeping the above facts in mind, *garbhaadhaan* is considered a *dhaarmika* duty to be performed after receiving the blessings of gods and goddesses and the elders in the family.

2. Pumsavan Samskaar

When conception is two-three months old and the outward signs of pregnancy are visible, the ritual of *pumsavan* is observed. In fact, three months after conceiving, the physical characteristics of the foetus start developing. Its limbs and brain begin to develop, as also its mental features. There is immense influence of the parents' mind and character on the foetus. Therefore, to make the baby both physically and mentally strong, this ritual is very important according to Hindu scriptures. Two basic reasons for performing this ceremony are given.

First is to beget a son and the second is to ensure a healthy, beautiful and intelligent child with excellent character. Referring to the first lesson, it is mentioned in *Smrti Samgraha:* गर्भाद् भवेच्च पुंसूते पुंस्त्वस्यप्रतिपादनम् (*garbhaad bhaveccha pumsoote pumstvasyapratipaadanam*), meaning "may a strong and healthy male child be born, hence this *pumsavan* ritual is being performed." *Manu-Smrti* (9/138), mentions in detail about this ritual — पुन्नाम्नो नरकाद्यस्मात् त्रायते पितरं सुतः (*punnaamno narakaadyasmaat traayate pitaraṁ sutah*), meaning, the one who releases one's ancestors from Pum, the wicked hell, is alone called a son. Therefore, in order to escape from hell, a male progeny is wished for.

In the words of Manu Maharaj — गर्भाद् भवेच्च पुंसूते पुंस्त्वस्यप्रतिपादनम् (*garbhaad bhaveccha pumsoote pumstvasyapratipaadanam*), meaning, "may a strong and male child (and not a female child) develop in the womb." This is the result of *pumsavan* ritual.

Explaining this *pumsavan* ritual in detail, scriptures mention that this rite is meant to give spiritual strength to the mother.

People who believe in the power of Vedas and *mantras* and perform this *pumsavan* ritual, produce a desire in the mother's mind to have a male child.

The aim of *pumsavam* ritual is also to help in obtaining a strong and healthy progeny. This ritual helps in protecting the unborn child in the womb, and ensures that the child is bestowed with the best character and traits. Simultaneously, it is prayed that the child is not only strong and healthy but should also be born fully developed on completion of the full gestation period. By this ritual the mother and father take a vow to ensure proper physical development of the foetus.

There is a lot of controversy over this ceremony's aim to have a male progeny in preference to a girl child, but the main purpose of the ritual to beget a progeny which is strong bodily, mentally and spiritually, cannot be challenged.

3. Seemantonnayan Samskaar

This ritual is performed during the fourth, sixth or eighth month of pregnancy. Its aim is to purify the womb through *mantras*, boost the morale of the mother, and induce her to have good and pure thoughts in her mind. This ritual helps in averting miscarriage as Lord Indra's lightning power is very strong during the fourth, sixth and eighth months. Interesting to note is that after the completion of four months, the foetus's limbs and heart begin to grow. There is development in the physical and psychological aspects as well. During this time, the sense of awareness for the unborn child starts developing in the mind of the mother-to-be. The foetus develops consciousness and is ready to absorb thoughts and teachings from outside of the womb. This is the time when only good deeds are discussed with the mother to keep her happy and cheerful so that only good and noble thoughts and words impact the unborn child. This is the stage of the unborn child which is very sensitive and it immediately absorbs the mood of the mother.

This happened with Kayaadhu, the mother of Prahlaad, the divine child. When Devarishi Naarad narrated the Bhagavad *bhakti* tales to her, Prahlaad listened to the whole tales when he was still in his mother's womb. Simultaneously, Sukhdev, the son of Vyasa received the whole knowledge when he was in his mother's womb, and even when Arjun was explaining to his wife Subhadraa about the *chakravyooh*'s penetration (a battle manoeuvre), Arjun's son Abhimanyu listened to it while being in his mother's womb.

4. Jaatkarm Samskaar

This ritual is performed after the child has been born but before the umbilical cord is severed. Prayers for the child's health, wealth and strength are recited with proper *mantra*s. With a golden spoon or any other small utensil, the child is fed a little honey and ghee amidst prayers for his protection performed with *shloka*s recitation.

Initially, when the child is in the womb, the three rituals mentioned above are performed. This fourth ritual is performed after the birth of the child along with the recitation of proper *mantra*s and *shloka*s. Six drops of ghee along with honey is given to the new-born baby. After severing of the umbilical cord the father performs a *yagya* and whispers nine *mantra*s in the right or the left ear of the baby, and prays for his fame, energy, knowledge, health, wealth and a long life. After this, the ritual of breastfeeding by the mother begins, followed by eulogizing the gods and goddesses and culmination of the *yagya*. After this, for ten days, in the house where the baby is born oblations of boiled rice and yellow mustard seeds are put in the *yagya* fire. This ritual is done to ward off evil spirits, diseases and germs, and destroy them so that the new-born is blessed with only pious and pure atmosphere all around.

5. Naamkaran Samskaar

Smriti Samgraha mentions,

> आयुर्वर्चोऽभिवृद्धिश्च सिद्धिर्व्यवहृतेस्तथा ।
> नामकर्मफलं त्वेतत् समुद्दिष्टं मनीषिभिः ॥
>
> *aayurvarcho 'bhivriddhischa*
> *siddhirvyavahritestathaa* ।
> *naamkarmaphalam tvetat*
> *samuddishtam maneeshibhih* ॥
>
> *meaning*, the name-giving ceremony is performed to bless the child, give him a new name, and wish for his long life with fame and glory. His personality gets overhauled and undergoes total reshaping.

The ceremony is performed generally on the tenth day of child-birth. As per his name, his appearance and his deeds begin to form slowly. Every human being contains a part (character) of a man, a cow, a horse, a bird, a *rishi*, his ancestors, a demi-god, a demon, etc. But he contains the soul of only a human being within him, and therefore, is called a human being. The *Parashara Grihyasutra* mentions, दशम्यामुत्थाप्य पिता नाम करोति (*dashamyaamutthaapya pitaa naama karoti*). Sometimes after completion of ten days of child birth, the mother is purified through *yagya* and this ceremony is performed. At some places, the name-giving ceremony is done after the completion of one hundred days of child birth, while at some other places after the completion of one year of child-birth. According to the followers of *Gobhila Grihyasutra*, जननादृशरात्रे व्युष्टे शतरात्रे संवत्सरे वा नामधेयकरणाम् (*jananaadrisharaatre vyushte shatraatre samvatsare vaa naamadheya-*

karanaam). In this ritual, after feeding of honey and ghee to the child, amidst the whisper of sweet and wise words into his ears, the sun worship is done. It is prayed that this child be as bright and glowing as the sun. The earth is also paid obeisance and the ceremony is concluded. After this, the child's head is turned towards the northern direction with his feet to the south. Several gifts are exchanged, and a new name given to the child. Amidst the chanting of his new name, all the people assembled pray for his good health, wealth, prosperity and a long life.

In earlier times, the name of the child followed the names of great sages, gods, etc. so that the child could follow in their footsteps and become powerful and achieve fame like them. It is a very common psychological phenomenon and a fact that when a person is called by a particular name, he inherits the qualities of that person only. When a person is called by name *ghatiyaa* (a low-quality person), he will inherit the low-quality effects in him, always causing hindrance in his progress and bringing him discouragement. Thus, the child's name should be such that it "boosts" energy into him and his confidence grows.

Usually, there are three bases that are followed during the naming ceremony. First, his name must follow his birth-star so that he could be identified by that star easily. Also, his name should begin with any letter which applies to that particular star. This helps in identifying both his name and star under which he is born; besides it becomes easy for the astrologers to prepare his horoscope without much problem. Basically, to understand the details about a person's name, this is the only scientific source people believe in. Secondly, the name should be such that helps in identifying the purpose of one's life on this earth. Finally, the third basis is that the name should be such that signifies your caste, lineage, and the family you belong to.

6. Nisraman Samskaar

Nishkraman means taking the child out of the house. The ceremony of taking the child out of the house is performed on an auspicious day, especially when both parents of the child are going out on a pilgrimage. This ritual helps in good health and longer life of the child when the blessings of sages and scholars are bestowed on him —

निष्क्रमणादायुषो वृद्धिरप्युद्दिष्टा मनीषिभिः ।

nishkramanaadaayusho vriddhirapyuddishtaa maneeshibhih ।

The ceremony is usually performed in the fourth month after the child's birth when his senseorgans have been developed so as to face the natural surroundings with heat and air all around. Both the sun and the moon are worshipped, and the child made to look at both of them. This ritual is the main reason for holding this ceremony. Since man is made of five elements — ether, air, fire, water and earth — the father of the child wishes that the blessing of all these five substances be bestowed on his child for his good health and welfare.

शिवे तेस्तां द्यावापृथिवी असंतापे अभिश्रियौ, शं ते सूर्य
आ तप तुशं वातु ते हृदे । शिवा अभि क्षरं त्वापो
दिव्याः पयस्वतीः ॥ — अथर्ववेद सं. 8.2.14

shive testaam dyaavaaprithivee
asamtaape abhishriyou,
sham te soorya aa tapa tusham vaatu te hride ।
shivaa abhi ksharam tvaapo divyaah payasvateeh ॥
— *Atharvaveda*, Sam. 8.2.14

meaning, O child! May the universe and the earth shower blessings on you. May your heart always be the abode of fresh and clean air. May the pious rivers, the Ganga and the Yamuna, bring clean and tastier water for you.

7. Annapraashan Samskaar

The child's stomach may have developed some infection from unclean food from his mother when in the womb. Therefore, to clean it and to start giving him solid food is why the ritual called *annapraashan* is performed. About six or seven months after birth teeth begin to grow and the digestive system becomes active. The child's body and mind develop according to the food he consumes. Our thinking, emotions, expectations, the inner consciousness, and much more, all depend on food only. It's from food that we get the elementary substances which help in forming blood, skin, etc. to run our lives smoothly.

In the sixth month after a child's birth, the ceremony of first partaking of solid food must be performed. Our *shastra*s mention that food is the life of all beings. *Gita* mentions that it is the food only which forms our mind. Therefore, food has a very great importance in our life. Consuming pure, nourishing and virtuous food keeps our mind and body healthy. Food is the probable cause for most physical and mental illnesses, leading to the deterioration of the mind.

The ritual of *annapraashan,* initiates the child in the consumption of purified, healthy and nourishing food. The aim of this ritual is to make the child energetic, strong and judicious through food. As such, food made in ghee or mixed with curd, honey and ghee is consumed in this ritual. After almost six months, the child is able to digest semi-solid foods. Therefore, it is due to this very reason that the ritual is performed in the sixth month. During this ritual, only light but healthy food is given that can be digested easily and make the child strong. *Mantra*s are recited and the oblation of food is made to the deities. Upanishads have warned us never to criticize, dishonour, condemn or abuse the food at any time. They even are against throwing away the food, serving the leftover food, or expecting to consume the same, etc. and all these are to be condemned. Food is life, and one should never misuse it.

Killing another living being for flesh to keep alive one's body is not justified at all. Consuming the flesh of other living beings is a crime which directly affects the mind. Cruel thoughts like terror, torture, fear, intolerance, etc. enter our mind, which ultimately affect its spiritual growth. Intoxicating materials also spoil a mind. Consuming liquor, narcotics, etc. is totally banned in our *shastra*s. Man is by nature a vegetarian. Therefore, by consuming only vegetarian food, he can prolong his age, strengthen his power and increase his energy. Consuming non-vegetarian food is totally prohibited for him. But today, man is not giving serious thought to nutritious food which is leading him to serious mental and physical problems. To practise meditation it is essential that a man should keep both his mind and body pure. Regarding food, it is said that one must always consume clean and beneficial food, lesser food and food that has been earned by true service only, i.e. *hitabhuka, mitabhuka, ritabhuka*! with all these perspectives in mind the *annapraashan* ceremony is performed.

8. Vidyaarambh Samskaar

Gaining knowledge from teachers and studying the Vedas and Upanishads is the main purpose of this ritual. When the minds of both boys and girls are mature enough to grasp knowledge, this ritual is performed. Usually, a child who has reached five years of age is eligible to go through this ritual. With the blessings of Lord Ganesh, the Lord of Prosperity, and Goddess Sarasvati, the Goddess of Knowledge, this ritual is begun.

Knowledge is the only means to spiritual progress. Our scriptures mention two kinds of knowledge. One is the knowledge (in general) which helps in amassing wealth and earning name and fame in society. This is called *avidyaa* or "non-knowledge." The second is the true knowledge (the divine knowledge or *vidyaa*) that helps the man grow his mental powers, keeping away from worldly pleasures and being contented with meeting his barest minimum needs. Both these types of knowledge have played prominent roles in our life. There is a scriptural saying — सा विद्या या विमुक्तये (*saa vidyaa yaa vimuktaye*), meaning, knowledge is one that gives salvation. All the rest is *avidyaa* or ignorance. This knowledge leads to wisdom and its possession earns one *mukti,* i.e. liberation or salvation. In Vedas, it is mentioned — ऋते ज्ञानान्न मुक्ति (*rite jnaanaanna mukti*) meaning, without wisdom salvation is not possible. Therefore, gaining wisdom is the only way to spiritual development. The other knowledge, the second one, is ignorance or illusory knowledge, which leads to action, and this also in turn earns wisdom. Without any action, wisdom is lame; and without wisdom, any action is blind and foolish. When both wisdom and actions meet, man gets salvation. The importance of both has been accepted and highlighted in *Ishavasya Upanishad.*

> The person who simultaneously has both these — knowledge (containing wisdom) and ignorance (containing action) — overcomes death through action and attains immortality through wisdom together and understands the true reality, both ignorance (from action) and knowledge (from wisdom) simultaneously.

This important ceremony, the beginning of impartation of knowledge, should be done according to Vedic rites so that the child becomes cultured and wise. He should keep this goal in mind at all times and without being influenced by the current environment and surroundings, he should study the Vedas and Upanishads under a learned *guru* and become spiritually enlightened. To inculcate such a spirit this ritual is very essential as it keeps him aware and awake about his goal and makes him understand the ways leading to the attainment of wisdom.

9. Choodaakarma (mundan) Samskaar

In this ritual, the child's head is tonsured for the first time with the help of a razor. After the child-birth, between the end of first year and before the completion of third year, usually this ritual is performed. According to Hindu belief if a child's head is tonsured within a year of his birth, it would have a negative effect on his health and may bring ill-luck for all. Following customs some families perform this ritual on fifth or seventh year of the child as well.

The importance of this ritual is mainly to strengthen the child's brain, increase its capacity and ability, and remove any impure characteristics which might have impacted his brain when he was in the womb. The result and effects of this ritual increase the knowledge, energy, life and fame of the child. This ritual is usually performed in a temple or at some place of pilgrimage because the serene atmosphere at these places has a very healthy effect on the child. It is believed that along with the shorn hair the impure thoughts in his brain also fall out, and pure and virtuous thoughts enter his brain.

According to the Aashvalaayana Grihyasutra,
तेन ते आयुषे वपामि सुश्लोकाय स्वस्तये ।

— आश्वलायन गृह्यसूत्र 1.17.12

tena te aayushe vapaami sushlokaay svastaye ।
— *Ashlaayana Grihyasutra* 1.17.12

meaning, choodaakarma (*mundan*) ritual leads to long life, and the child gains beauty and grows into a benevolent being.

It is notable that this *choodaakarma* ritual is basically the worship of brain only. Using the brain to its fullest use and rationally is wisdom. The person who performs auspicious and charitable deeds is rewarded, but a person who always has negative feelings of harming others is punished accordingly by God. The person who develops ideas of troubling others, himself gets unbalanced and loses his control. This ritual is performed so that the mind remains cool and is put to good use always.

The above-mentioned nine ceremonies are called *dosh maarjan samskaar*, by completing which the seed or foetus in the womb is purified and the new-born child's sins, accrued from previous births, are destroyed. Therefore, these rituals are also known as *shodhak samskaar* (the purificatory rituals).

After having cleaned and removed all the evil effects on the newborn child, seven more rituals are performed to awaken his hidden talents which are present inside him. These rituals are called *gunaadhaan samskaar* (character-infusing rituals) or the *anuvrat samskaar* (complying or obeying rituals) or even the *atishayaadhaan samskaar* (ritual giving surprising results) as these help the individual to imbibe all good and extraordinary qualities. All these rituals are performed under the guidance of an *aacaarya* or *purohit* only. These rituals help in building the self-confidence of the child.

10. Karnavedh Samskaar

This is a ceremony of piercing of the ears, which takes place between six and sixteen months of the child-birth or when the child is three or five years of age or at a suitable time according to family custom. This ritual is performed to confer womanhood or manhood on a child. It is a belief that the sun's rays enter the body of the child through the holes on the earlobes and infuse energy. After this ritual the girls can wear jewellery. The ritual also helps in protecting the child from diseases as is done in the acupuncture system.

According to Sushruta, **रक्षा भूषणनिमित्तं बालस्य कर्णोविध्येते** (*rakshaa bhooshananimittam baalasya karnovidhyete*), with the growth of the child, the jewellery in the ears helps in giving protection to the child which is the belief according to this ritual. Girls wear jewellery in the ears to beautify themselves. They also get their nose pierced so that they can wear jewellery in their nose also. The custom is to pierce both the ears. Followers of Sushruta say the maximum benefit of this ritual is only attained when the piercing of the ears is done on its lower side or upper side which helps in gaining inner peace. Further it is mentioned that an expert physician should hold with his left hand the ear of the child firmly, and with a sharp needle pierce it. All this should be done directly under the glare of the sun's rays entering into the ear. Later, the physician should similarly pierce the other ear too. The right ear gives *brahma-shakti*, or knowledge or mental power. While the left ear gives *kshaatra-shakti* or physical power. Therefore, this ritual helps the child attain both the powers and make him an expert in scriptures and weapon-use so that he can protect his people and rule the country with righteousness.

Our scriptures mention that a person who has not got his ears pierced through this ritual, cannot ever perform *shraaddh* (a ceremony for honouring the deceased). The ears of a brahman or vaishya, under this ritual, are pierced by a silver needle; that of shudra, by an iron needle; and that of kshatriya, by a golden needle only. To keep our brain energized from all sides, piercing of nose and the ears on both sides, and wearing golden jewellery, is recommended. Wearing a nose ring prevents nasal diseases and keeps cough and cold away. Whereas wearing earrings helps women normalize their menstrual periods, this gives protection from diseases like hysteria as well.

11. Yajnopaveet (Upanayana) Samskaar

According to Manu —

> मातुरग्रेऽधिजननं द्वितीयं मौञ्जिबन्धनं
>
> — मनुस्मृति 2.169
>
> *maaturagre 'dhijananam*
> *dviteeyam maunjibandhanam* ।
>
> — *Manu-Smrti* 2.169
>
> *meaning*, the first birth of the child is from the mother's womb and second birth is through this *yajnopaveet* ritual, which means wearing a girdle made of *moonj* grass (*maunji*).

A child born from his mother's womb always carries the results of good and bad deeds done in his previous births. By the help of this *yajnopaveet* ritual, he can wipe out all the bad effects and retain only the good effects of his *karma*s. This is known as his second birth. The brahmans, the kshatriyas and vaishyas are called "twice-born" as they all undergo this ritual. According to Manu, without *yajnopaveet*, nobody is entitled to perform any religious ceremonies.

After the solemnization of this ceremony only, the child is entitled to take part in any religious rituals. When a person gets the right to perform all kinds of *yagya*s, it is called the *yajnopaveet* ritual. Wearing a *yajnopaveet* (white sacred thread) means a person carries on his shoulders the responsibilities of understanding and following all human, natural and divine laws with a view to obtaining the grace of God. It is mentioned in the *Padma Purana*'s Kaushal Kanda that evil deeds done knowingly and unknowingly in crores of years get destroyed by wearing *yajnopaveet*. According to *Parashara-Grihya-Sutra* 2.2.7, just like Indra was given by Brihaspati a *yajnopaveet* (sacred thread) for his protection, similarly, to enhance age, power, knowledge and wealth, it is always wise to wear *yajnopaveet*. It also purifies the character of a person and gives him confidence to face the most difficult of the tasks and overcome it very easily. By wearing this sacred thread, all beings attain a higher status, i.e. from human form to saintly form. This ritual brings a physical change in youth, who now thinks very high and nobly about the welfare of all and promises to follow these ideals throughout his life. After this promise only, the second innings of his life starts. This is called the "second life" (or twice born) and the promises made during this ritual's performance and fulfilling them, help the person gain higher spiritual powers.

Dvij means the second birth, i.e. twice-born. After performing this ritual, the person foregoes all his animal-like instincts and childhood activities and pledges to become a very responsible person and look after the welfare of the society and mankind. He takes a pledge that he will rise above all beings sacrificing all his passions and desires and work for the welfare of people only. Taking a pledge of this kind itself is like attaining a new birth and is regarded very sacred under the Indian traditions. In this particular situation, this ritual of *yajnopaveet* takes place so that the person is reminded time and again about his pledge and his duties whenever he sees his *yajnopaveet* (white sacred thread over his left shoulder). Such persons who undergo this ritual are called *dvij* or the second-born persons.

This *yajnopaveet* ritual basically is the principle under which a person undergoing a disciplined life is made to become self-independent. This ritual has chiefly a direct relation with the *gurukul* (school) also. When a child is sent to the school for the first time, the teacher after going through his introduction, tonsures his head. The child is later given clothes, a sacred thread and a wooden staff, and asked to adopt the *brahmacharya* system of education. The child is asked to perform a *yagya* where he is explained very clearly about his duties, the rules of the school, about his keeping cleanliness, restriction on speaking and avoidance of sleeping during the day, etc. After this, the teacher whispers the *Gayatri mantra* three times into the ears of the student. The student reciprocates by taking the blessings of the teacher and asks for alms from his teacher. The teacher places something in the hands of his student, who entrusts it back to the teacher. After the successful completion of this ritual only, the teacher begins the lessons on *veda-adhyan* or the study of scriptures. This ritual is followed even today as per the *gurukul* (school) style at many places.

On completion of the *gurukul* phase successfully, the other rituals are performed. But today these rituals are not performed as per ancient traditions, but remain for namesake only as they hardly have any importance in our daily life.

12. Vedaarambh Samskaar

The ritual of *vedaarambh* is similar to the previous ritual of *yajnopaveet* (*upanayan*) where the teacher after making his student undergo the *yajnopaveet* ritual and taking a pledge from him to lead a disciplined life, would share the knowledge of Vedas with him. The students who were unable to lead a disciplined life were not imparted this knowledge because there was the likelihood of misuse of this knowledge as they would be unable to understand the relevance and depth of this knowledge and may take it lightly and not seriously. This was the reason a student was asked to first undergo eleven other rituals and prepare himself, both mentally and physically, before understanding the secret of Veda knowledge and acknowledging it seriously.

The meaning of Veda is in fact knowledge, i.e. knowledge is Veda. The four Indian Vedas are not only the invaluable treasures of Indian civilization but they are also the most ancient warehouse of knowledge of the world. They are considered to be the most ancient scriptures of the world and contain and explain in depth the fundamental principles of creation, the mode of creating it, life of a human being, misfortune — the reason and remedies to get rid of them — the spiritual development, etc. The various religions and sects of the world reflect the basic principles of these Vedas only. To learn such a deep and vast knowledge, the above ritual needs to be practised thoroughly.

There are three kinds of distresses — spiritual, physical and divine distress. Amongst these, the spiritual distress is the most important. The other two are only its subsidiaries. The reason for being in spiritual distress is only illiteracy and ignorance. Man does not understand the law of nature and creation. Nature does not harm any being, but it is only man who works against it and calls for troubles. This is his ignorance and a solution to overcome it must be sought out. It is due to this ignorance that man develops weak features in his body like attachment, passion, desire, etc. which force him to go against nature and face its consequences. All these result in trouble and cause distress only. The solution to get rid of all these troubles lies in our Vedas only. Therefore, one can attain salvation only by accessing them and studying them. Knowledge is the only means to end our distress. It is mentioned in the Vedas — ऋेत ज्ञानान्न मुक्तिः (*rite jnaanaanna muktih*), meaning "knowledge is the only means to salvation"; न हि ज्ञानेन सदृशं पवित्रमिह विधते (*na hi jnaanena sadrisham pavitramiha vidhate*), meaning "there is no other commodity in the world which can be at par with knowledge."

Therefore, recitation of Vedas is very important and is given a higher position in our lives, making it a part and parcel of our rituals. It contains rituals for all castes and is immediately followed after the ritual of *yajnopaveet.*

In the beginning a *yagya* is performed and the child is asked to recite the *Gayatri mantra.* The child is explained the meaning of this *Gayatri mantra*, along with the usefulness of the staff, clothes and a sacred thread which were given to him earlier. Their importance is explained to him in detail. After the completion of this ritual, the student asks for alms from his teacher (*guru*). On receiving alms from his teacher, the student dedicates the same to his *guru*. The teacher takes a little out of it and the remainder is returned to his student. Later the *yagya* is completed and the student takes blessing from his teacher. Then begin his actual Veda classes, preaching the knowledge of Vedas.

13. Keshaant Samskaar

This ritual, meaning cutting of hair, is also a part of schooling. This ritual is done at the age of 16 followed by *samaavartan samskaar,* also called the *snaan samskaar.* After the completion of this ritual the student is considered to have graduated as a complete Brahman after attaining total education from his teacher. This ritual is the time to bid goodbye to the *gurukul* (school) and welcome a new life of *grihasth-aashram* (the second or domestic stage of life) and enter his home once again. He gets his head shaved before this ritual. The ritual of shaving of his head is also perfomed in a similar way to the *mundan* ceremony performed earlier.

14. Samaavartan Samskaar

This ritual is done to make the students aware of his divine powers. After the completion of all the above rituals, there is a great mental development in the student. He becomes more polite, humble, kind, helpful and responsible towards his duties and thinks of serving his society and working for the nation's benefit. He puts in his everything to carry out his duties and fulfil his ambitions. He does not run after the luxuries, but instead goes for the realized world and achieves his target.

Our education has today helped us gain all the physical and material comforts and made our life so very easy. But this very education has failed to develop the knowledge of an individual and make even one perfect human being. Therefore, to call this education as "perfect" would be illogical. The main aim of any education should be to work for the benefit of a human being and help in his development. With this in view India adopted these rituals so that a student understands them and becomes a responsible citizen of this country. Before leaving his *aashram*, the student is thoroughly examined and tested by the teacher so that once in his own home the student should understand all his responsiblities and become a very noble citizen and work for the welfare of the society only.

In today's education we do not see any ideal of that kind. There are no more those teachers who could discipline the students — in fact, no discipline exists anywhere either among teachers or among students.

This ritual performance is the beginning of his consecration or preparation for a religions ceremony. After the completion of this ritual successfully, he is allowed to independenty think about his own self and hence start a married life.

15. Paanigrahan (vivaah) Samskar

There was no marriage-like ritual at the time creation began. The rule as to who can marry whom did not exist. Anybody could have sexual relationship with any person of his or her choice and produce offsprings. In the absence of a clear way of knowing the identity of a child's actual father, the mother's importance gained prominence and the children began to be recognized by their mothers' names only. Father was no more important. This system went on up to the Vedic period, but was soon strongly opposed by the sages inhabiting the mountain tops. They considered such relations bestial and made new marriage laws. Our traditional Sanskrit Smritis and Sutras mention eight different kinds of marriages. They are: Brahma, Daiva, Aarsha, Prajapatya, Asura, Gandharva, Raakshasa and Paishaach. Amongst these, the initial four are more popular in marriage performance while the other four are less popular. The Brahma type is more popular in solemnizing marriages between two castes and therefore, all its ritualistic observances have been carefully scripted and adhered to.

For the upliftment, security, multiplication and prosperity of one's community and family, the society supported marriages within one's own clan and community only. The ritual makers framed special rules and regulations and enforced them strictly. Thus, from here began the caste system which divided the whole society into four major castes — Brahman, kshatriya, vaishya and shudra. Each family was recognized by these castes only. Children who were born from cross-caste relationships, were put in a separate sub-caste because neither of the families accepted them. In this way the four major castes went on dividing and sub-dividing into further smaller sub-castes. Since the people from each of these four castes had phenomenally developed their manners and talents, they began to be distinguished by that particular caste only. Rules were framed so that people of one caste should get their children married in that particular caste only so that their community progresses, family multiplies and ultimately their coming generations are secured. Besides, maintaining illegal relations and having sex with people from the other castes was prohibited. People who protected their caste, clan, and religion but still preferred to have children of another caste or clan were given the permission to marry in that caste.

In *Manu-Smriti* it is mentioned that a brahman is allowed to marry a girl of any caste (*Manu-Smrti* 3.13) in the interest of the society and community. But the brahman who is a follower of the *grihastha-aashram,* is not allowed to marry the daughter of a shudra (lower caste) even though there may be any amount of emergency (*Manu-Smrti* 3.14). Marriages can be possible considering the higher status of another family, clan or community, but it is always advisable to arrange marriages within the same caste only. This will not only enhance the chances of retaining family characteristics and traditions but also it will increase their population and physical strength. Chances of religious tolerance and respect for both will also increase.

It has been mentioned in our scriptures that after seven generations of marriages the woman will stop forming blood relationships. A remedy to this can be worked out temporarily, but its permanent results have to be faced. Man can break rules and amend them but the consequent results cannot be avoided. This is clearly mentioned in several religious texts and books. Therefore, the rules which have been framed for protecting the caste should be followed religiously by man and this becomes his duty. It has been mentioned in *Manu-Smrti* (3.27) that when a learned and cultured bridegroom is adorned with clothes and ornaments and is given a suitable bride in marriage it is called *Brahma Vivaah*.

In the same chapter, in *sutra* 5, it has also been mentioned that where relations (matrimonial) have not occurred in the last seven generations, either from her mother's (*supinda*) or her father's side, to marry such a girl is considered very ideal. Here in *sutra*s 12-13, it has been further mentioned that a twice-born (*dvijaati*) person should marry a person from the similar caste only. Here the *dvijaati* caste only means: the brahman, kshatriya, and vaishya. It has no concern with the castes that exist today. In our religious scriptures, we find several rules and remedies that have been given and by following them one can protect himself, his clan and his religion. This will help him to develop his religion further and make him physically and mentally much more stronger and healthier.

All these marriages are being performed following several rules and rituals mentioned in various scriptures. If followed strictly, one can protect his clan, community and religion, and work for their upliftment.

On the occasion of marriages, several rites and rituals are being followed. The most important among these is the *paanigrahan* (*vivaah*) ritual, and this should be performed with total faith. An intelligent and well-mannered housewife can enhance the name and fame of her family by giving birth to well-cultured progenies. She can also utilize her intelligence and work for the benefit of the nation as well. Therefore, marriages are not merely "the performance of certain rituals" only. They help in uniting two totally different cultures and two souls, where husband and wife take a vow to lead a very peaceful and happy life. They are bound in a sacred relationship where both pledge to develop their family. To bring them emotionally closer is the aim of this ritual and not for having mere sexual pleasure only.

In the ancient days, there used to be ten different rituals and rites that were performed to solemnise any marriage. These ten rituals were: (1) bathing of both the bride and the groom; (2) warmly welcoming the groom; (3) gifting a cow; (4) gift of a girl in marriage; (5) the ceremony of exchanging clothes and gifts; (6) performance of *yagya;* (7) *paanigrahan;* (8) *shilaarohan* and *laajaahom;* (9) *saptapati;* (10) and Surya Dhruva and Arundhati *darshana.* Besides these, many other rituals which were prevalent in the society were also included in the marriage ceremony. Though these rituals were held differently in different societies, their goal was the same and their performing technique was also the same.

After the successful completion of all these ceremonies, the mutual love and affection between the bride and groom grows and becomes more strong. The dedication in performing this ritual is itself very sacred and undivided. It is, therefore, seen that before taking the vows before the God of Fire, a sacred knot is tied between the bride and the groom. On completion of taking all these vows, and both the bride and the groom having agreed to abide by them by giving their mutual consent, the knot is loosened as it is no longer required now. This is followed by the groom taking his bride to his home.

After the completion of marriage rites, several other social customs are also followed which may vary from caste to caste, and region to region. All of them have one common goal — to create an atmosphere of love and reverence, and have peace and gaiety all around. To attain good health, wealth, peace, prospertiy and total brotherhood, it is required that this ritual is performed with devotion and dedication.

After explaining in brief the sixteen rituals to the readers, mention is being made later in this book about other social rituals and customs practised in the *paanigrahan* (*vivaah*) ritual.

16. Agniparigrah Samskaar

Agniparigrah samskaar or the funeral ceremony is the ultimate ritual in a person's life. Placing fire on the body, or encircling the body with fire, is called *agniparigrah*. It is written in the scriptures that if a dead person is bidden farewell with all the proper rites and ceremonies, his soul becomes free from all desires and rests in peace in the heavens. A person who is not given proper farewell, without proper rites, leaves his desires unfulfilled and his soul never rests in peace and wanders and haunts for a very long period of time. Therefore, it is very essential to perform, with proper care, all the last rites for a dead person. This ritual is also called by the name *antyeshti samskaar.* This ritual is performed so that the dead person is freed from all family bondages, desires and demands. Prayers are made so that the passage of the soul may be easy and it can take a new birth without much trouble. The *sadgurus*, saints and sages do not require this ritual as they are already immortal, free from all sorts of desires or demands.

It has been mentioned in *Chudamanya Upanishad* that *Brahman* gave birth to the soul; soul to ether; ether to air; air to fire; fire to water; and finally water to earth. Our body is made with the help of these five elements only. In Hindu religion at the funeral ceremony, the body is offered to the fire so that it is once again mingled with the five elements: ether, air, water, fire and earth, of which it was originally made of.

This is merely a ritual and a part of death ritual (*kriyaakarma*). The ceremony that is being performed to offer the body to fire and bid it farewell forever peacefully is called the *agniparigrah samskaar.* Apart from this, the rituals of ancestor worship like *pindadaan, aashouch, paalan, shraadh karma*, etc. that are being performed later are merely part of this *kriyaa* (ceremony) only and not part of any other separate ritual.

The meaning of these rituals is basically of two kinds as has already been mentioned above. The first is to free a person from all bondages — from his faults and sins that may have been committed by him earlier. The second meaning is संस्कारो गुणान्तराधानम् इति संस्कारः (*samskaaro gunaa-ntaraadhaanam iti samskaarah*), meaning conceptualizing the ritual and meditating over it, which is also a ritual on its own. When any element is put in the fire, it becomes pure. When the soul leaves the body, the body begins to decay. Therefore it is consigned to the flames and reduced to ashes. The body has been purified and freed from all the sins. Completing the funeral ceremony with all the rites and rituals helps the soul attain to heavens and rest in peace. Fire is ardent and full of lights. So is the soul. That these two lights should merge into that all-powerful light is the only purpose for which people perform the funeral ceremony religiously.

Man is made up of three separate bodies. The first body is the *sthool shareer* (the tangible body or the physical body); the second body is the *sookshma shareer* (subtle body); and the third body is the *kaaran shareer* (the causal body), which is the seed of the body. The subtle body is controlled by the mind in which previous life's actions and memories are stored. To purify the mind and body of the deceased, this ceremony is performed. At the time of funeral, whatever rites are being performed, have a direct effect on the subtle body. When death occurs, the subtle body moves around the corpse of the deceased only. So whatever rites are performed on and with the corpse, they directly affect the subtle body and remain around till the corpse has been burnt completely. After the funeral ceremony has been completed, the subtle body returns satisfied. This ritual plays a very vital role at the time of the funeral ceremony on the subtle body (*sookshma shareer*) and hence is counted as one of the sacraments. Similarly, the rites that involve work, emotions, etc. that are contributed by other people, also have a direct effect on the subtle body.

A person who is very angry is pacified with polite words, and he forgets his temper immediately, in the same way this soul, when rites are perfomed, is totally satisfied and starts on its next journey. In fact, rituals are being done only to purify the souls, pacify them and help them to remain cool and calm and in peace wherever they habitat. The tangible body (*sthool shareer*) has nothing to do with these rituals.

The subtle body (*sookshma shareer*) comprises 17 groups which are: the intellect, five matters, five senseorgans, five *praanas* (air) and mind, which remain in body till the time of salvation. This is the reason why subtle body is formed again and again only to be dismantled and formed again. Therefore, these rituals are for the purification of the subtle body only. Performed with proper care and dedication the feelings and emotions attached with the body get purified. Therefore, this is an important ceremony.

Before the corpse is put on the pyre for final cremation, other rituals like bathing the corpse; garlanding it with flowers; taking part in the funeral procession; use of coconut oil, sandalwood, ghee, saffron, etc.; lighting the pyre and making the whole environment pious and pure; recitation of *mantra*s and *shloka*s, etc. all have great effect on the subtle body. All these rites when combined purify the body totally — mentally, physically and spiritually. This is the ultimate ceremony in a man's life and should be performed by following proper rites and customs.

During the *antyeshti samskaar,* the head of the corpse should be on the northern direction when placed on the pyre and the feet must face the south. A pot of water is carried by the eldest son of the deceased. He places it on his left shoulder and circumambulates the corpse once. After completing one round, he drops the pot and breaks it near the head of the corpse. Last respects are paid by all relatives and friends who have gathered there. The body is then taken to the pyre platform and placed there. Ghee is poured in the mouth of the corpse and a small piece of sandalwood is placed on the body. After the recitation of *om agnaye svaahaa* and five other *mantra*s and offering ghee, the pyre is lit. At this time the God of Fire is requested to take the body towards heavens. The pyre is lit by the eldest son and the recitation of hymns and *shloka*s continues. After this, when the corpse is half burnt, the *kapaal kriyaa* (ceremonially breaking the skull of the corpse) is performed by the eldest son amidst the recitation of *mantra*s and ghee is poured on the side of the head first and then on the whole body again.

After the funeral ceremony is over, the soul remains active for ten days with the subtle body. On completion of the ten days of (*aashoucha*) impurity, it takes the form of a *preta* (spirit of the dead). When one year is complete it assumes a *pitradeh* (the body of a mane or ancestor). Therefore, for one whole year, the soul remains attached to this family only, and all ceremonies should be performed with full rites and rituals for one complete year, so that the soul is purified and is assured of a noble future when it accepts a new body and lives in it.

The soul is attached with this world due to ignorance only. It is this ignorance only that has formed our body and given to it a shape. As per our deeds that were performed in the previous births, our body takes a new shape. In order to get a good body and shape only, these rituals are performed. With death, only the body, which is physical, gets burnt. But the soul remains alive for generations to come. The soul takes a physical body depending upon our past deeds. When the body is in a human form, the tasks done by it should always be human. We can effect changes to this physical body by doing those deeds which will get rid of the sins and purify the actions done in our previous births. When the causal body or *kaaran shareer* gets released we call it *moksha* or salvation. "Cause" or *kaaran* is the seed of this body and the physical body is only its appearance and a reflection of the tasks that were performed in our previous birth. The soul wants to change its desires into actions and induces the physical body to do good and bad deeds because the soul cannot do anything without a medium, and that medium is the physical body. This physical body, therefore is also a part of the soul.

It is due to his ignorance that man is unable to understand the laws of creation, and he has therefore to take the help of scriptures in carrying out all his duties in this life. Man should not go astray following the doctrines of different religions, but instead should do all acts according to the custom and rules of his own religion, i.e. his *svadharma,* and aspire to lead a noble life. He should always follow his religion and work for its protection. *Bhagavad Gita* says — स्वधर्मे निधनं श्रेयः परधर्मो भयावहः (*svadharme nidhanam shreyah paradharmo bhayaavaha*).

In *Yajurveda* it is mentioned that persons who perform the last rites with proper rituals and respect using incenses and other fragrant materials, are considered very virtuous persons and they are seen often helping others. In fact, every person, in any time-period, should be given such a farewell with honour and respect with proper rites and rituals amidst the recitation of prayers, wishing for everyone's peace and welfare.

After obsequies, when the body has been reduced to ashes, washing of clothes, bathing, purifying the house, etc. takes place and prayers recited for giving peace to the deceased's soul. Prayers are also recited for each one's good health and prosperity. On the third day after cremation, the consigning of ashes takes place. They are either buried after digging a pit in the ground or they are immersed in the holy waters of river Ganges. According to the Arya Samaj sect followers, no rite is to be performed after this. They consider *shraaddha* (honouring the ancestors), *brahmabhoj* (community feeding), recitation of *Garuda Purana,* etc. as anti-Veda, but according to popular customs no harm will come if we conduct all these ceremonies. On the 10th, 11th and the 12th days, all the kith and kin of the deceased gather at one place and offer condolences. On the 13th day, the successor to the deceased is announced as per the custom prevailing in the family. It is believed that up to 12 days the deceased's subtle body remains inside the house. Therefore, on the 13th day, the successor is announced amidst the chanting of hymns. The water pitcher that was placed inside the house, is now taken out and given farewell with due rites in the presence of all the persons gathered inside the house. They all become witness to the culmination of this ceremony. The successor is given blessings by all the elders, and all present offer their best wishes for his hale, hearty and long life.

References

- *Manu-Smriti.*
- *Gita.*
- *Sushruta Samhitaa.*
- *Veda Vaakya.*
- *Smrti Samgraha.*
- *Brahmasutra.*
- *Ashvalaayan Grihyasutra.*
- *Parashara Grhyasutra.*
- *Gobhila Grihyasutra.*
- *Solah Samskaar.*
- *Hindu Reeti-Riwaaz.*
- *Solah Samskaar Vidhi.*
- *Hamaare Samskaar.*
- *Bhaaratiya Maanyeataayen.*

Sacred Customs and Rituals

The readers must have become familiar by now about the Sixteen Sacraments mentioned in brief earlier and that marriage ritual occupies an important place amongst them. The other rituals that have been mentioned are in a way related to this ceremony only. Marriage is considered a very significant ritual for giving society's sanction to a close relationship between a man and a woman as husband and wife. Therefore, it is also called a social system. A sweet and cordial atmosphere in the family, a loving relationship between husband and wife, healthy progenies, providing love and care to the children and seeing them grow as noble individuals — these are the main aims and features of this ceremony which is being followed since the Vedic times. The marriage ceremony is considered a sacrifice or an investiture ceremony since then. *Taittireeya Brahman* (2.2.2.6) mentions that a person who does not marry and enjoy family life, is a non-religious person devoid of any responsibilities in him. A person with a wife can only be called a duty-bound and responsible person. Any religious activity that is performed without a wife is never considered complete. A person who is unmarried has a lower position in society and gains less respect than a person who is married. Hence, the other aim of marriage can be said to be accomplishing religious tasks. Such views have been accepted in our social life also where the elders in the family insist that the marriage ceremony must be conducted with all rites and rituals.

Marriage is considered to be very sacred as it leads to physical and religious bonding between people in a community. It is for this reason the ceremony is given prominence with various hymns, rites and rituals attached, and is performed in a systematic way. Marriage creates a renewed sacred bond between husband and wife which must have existed between them in their past lives as well. Both husband and wife use all their energy and mind in having sexual relationship with a view to getting good progenies and together concentrate on improving their spiritual knowledge through self-control, self-sacrifice and self-confidence.

The marriage ceremony is the result of the combination of many rituals, based on information contained in scriptures like *Jyotish Shastra* (astrology), *Samaaj Shastra* (social customs), *Dharm* or *Vidhi Shastra* (religious rites), *Homa-anushthaan* (offering ablutions in fire), etc. besides many other commonly used religious texts. It also represents and reflects the social customs and practices that are prevalent in the society. It is said:

ब्याह तो केह्ये के मनै माण्डी ने देख,
घर केह्ये के मन्ने उधेडीन् देख . . . ।

byaah to kehye ke manai maandee ne dekh,
ghar kehye ke manne udhedeen dekh . . . ।

meaning, that this ceremony involves several social activities, practices and customs, on the completion of which not only the energy of a family increases but the enthusiasm and energy of the whole society multiplies several times.

It is the ideal time for rejoicing, singing songs, indulging in fun and frolic, attracting people, unrestrained humour, cracking jokes, etc. in all creating a merry and happy atmosphere all around.

Marriage rituals vary depending upon the community, the religion and the state where they are performed. But *paanigrahan* ritual is still considered as the most important. Marriage customs, rituals and rites among royal families are mentioned here — most of these rituals are followed by common people as well and are performed in the original or altered forms in the Indian society.

Search of Suitable Girl/Boy and Vaagdaan

This is the ritual of choosing a suitable boy and a suitable girl, to be united as husband and wife. Both see each other and give their acceptance to their own parents. Then the parents consider various factors and give a verbal decision to each other's family.

Before the marriage is solemnized, searching for a suitable match for a boy and a girl is essential. In earlier times, this responsibility was taken by a *pandit* or a family priest. But in the present times, with development and the high status societies, a suitable match is located by not only the *pandit*, family priests, relatives and friends, but also through advertisements in newspapers, magazines and periodicals, and matrimonial agencies which have sprung up everywhere. The internet also plays a significant part these days. Earlier, only the parents or the family elders saw the girl and the boy and took decisions. They did not consider it essential for arranging a meeting of the boy and the girl. As per the tradition prevalent among the Rajput families, they marry their children only within their own tribe or sect/group. For example, the Sisodiaas marry within Rathores or Bhaatee, Chauhaan, Sodaa, Kacchaavaa, Raanas of Nepal, or the Katoch family of Jammu only.

The father of the girl meets the boy's father and desires to send the horoscope of his daughter to the latter. If both families agree on this, then the girl's horoscope is sent, after consultation with the family priests, to the boy's house. The boy's family gets that horoscope compared with their boy's horoscope. Once the news about both horoscopes matching reaches the girl's house, the girl's family, to be very sure and satisfied, gets both the horoscopes compared and examined by their own family priests. After the family priests say that both the horoscopes match very well and give their approval, clearance is given for negotiation of a matrimonial alliance between the two families.

A photograph of the girl and her family details are sent to the boy's house. It is not essential that all the qualities of the boy should match with those of the girl. But it is said that the first and the foremost value or quality to be seen in a boy is his virtuous and cultured nature, and later follows his family and his finance; because if a boy is not virtuous and good, of what use is the family and its wealth? Both the parents and the relatives of the families meet and decide verbally on the dates for the preliminary functions, including engagement, and marriage. This ritual is called the *vaagdaan* (giving word) or the *kaul-vachan* (word of promise). When both sides agree, on an auspicious day relatives of the boy go to the girl's house for a meeting, and on this occasion, based on the horoscopes of the boy and the girl an auspicious time for the marriage is fixed.

In the present times, it is not only the parents and the relatives who take interest in matrimonial relations, but the boy and girl too are meeting and seeing each other. Both sides take the blessings from their family gods and goddesses and ancestors before the marriage date in solemnized. Since this is a very sensitive subject, it is not discussed in detail here.

Engagement Ceremony (Sagaai)

In this (*thahraav*) ceremony it is publicly announced that the boy and the girl are engaged ; and the usual ritual is to put a *tilak* (mark with sandal, *kumkum* and rice grain) on the forehead of the groom. The bride and the groom along with their families and relatives exchange some cash and gifts for the first time. On an auspicious day the *pandit* (brahman), from the side of the groom carries a coconut and a congratulatory message to the bride's family. Then the bride's family send their *pandit* (brahman) to the groom's house with a coconut and a congratulatory message. This ceremony is called *sagaaee* or *rokaa* (betrothal).

As per this *rokaa* ceremony, the bride's family invites the parents and the relatives of the groom to their house. Usually the groom's parents, sister, paternal aunt, a senior female relative (mother or grandmother), etc. go to the bride's place. Earlier, at the bride's place, all her family members and her relatives are present, besides the persons who finalized this matrimonial alliance.

The expanded form of the word *sagaa* means *sagaaee* (engagement) — meaning, the confluence of relationship with opulence or wealth. This ceremony is also called the *manganee* (asking in marriage). Nowadays, the bride and the groom exchange rings.

In the *Ramayan,* Raavan abducts Seetaa and confines her in the Ashok Vaatikaa. Raam sends his engagement ring to her to assure her and boost her morale. It was the engagement ring only which brought both Dushyant and Shakuntala together in Kalidasa's *Shaakuntalam*. Therefore, this ring has great significance even today. The engagement ceremony is only the beginning of the life of two unknown individuals together. It is celebrated with lots of fun and gaiety.

Betrothal Ceremony (teekaa)

This ceremony is usually held between 5 and 7 in the evening at the groom's house. The bride's family and their relatives customarily bring certain gifts for the groom and his relatives. These include coconuts and betelnuts (21 or 11), covered with gold or silver foil, buttons for the coat or a suit, a necklace with thick beads, a bracelet, a crescent, a light-weight gold chain, a ring, a wrist watch, a turban, a few *shagan* covers containing money, big steel plates (51 or 101) containing jaggery and various dry fruits, boxes of sweets, fruits and other items.

The ceremony is usually held in the main hall. Cushions are spread on the floor over a chequered cloth sheet. This is usually done by the elder brother or father of the bride. The material for the ceremonial worship is kept in a big silver plate which includes saffron, flowers, garlands, vermilion, rice, water pitcher, etc. A *teekaa* (small mark) is put on the forehead of the groom by the father of the bride. The groom is garlanded, given sweets and a betel (*paan*) is put into his mouth. He is presented a *siropaav* (a long robe from head to foot) and his family and the relatives are presented with various gifts. The groom seeks the blessings of all elders by bowing down before each one of them. The ceremony is then over and after some snacks and refreshments, the bride's parents and other family members and relatives take leave.

Gifts from the Groom's Side for the Bride

Earlier, before the betrothal or *teekaa* ceremony is performed, the groom's family which usually includes his elder sister, paternal aunt, mother, grand aunt, etc. take some gifts for the bride. This is called the *rokaa* ceremony, i.e. the bride is retained or engaged. The material that is taken along includes one or two sets of diamond necklaces, bangles, earrings set, two *saari*s or suits, several boxes of sweets, fruits, etc. The bride is asked to sit on a high platform. Groom's mother and elder sister put a *tilak* (small mark) on the forehead of the girl, sweetens her mouth and offers her *paan* (betel). On this occasion all elders give *shagan* (customary presents) to the girl. Later the bride bows before all elders and seeks their blessings.

The girls usually wear *saari*s or suits with lesser zari or lace work done on them.

Teej Festival Ritual

After the engagement ceremony and before the marriage occasion, if the festival of *teej* comes, from the groom's side, gifts are sent to the bride which include embroided *saari*s, bangles, some cash, sweets, etc. Usually the groom's younger brother or a close relative carry them to the bride's place. The bride's family welcomes them and honour them with *siropaav*s (long robe of honour) before bidding them farewell.

Marriage-paintings (Chittaram)

This ritual means decorating the walls, floors and doors of the houses with colourful paintings.

On the occasion of marriages it has been a very common practice of decorating both the bride and the groom's houses with various colourful paintings. This ritual is performed immediately after Vinaayakji (a small idol of Ganeshji) has been installed at a sacred place in both the houses. On the verandah, besides the decorations, paintings of various gods are put up and various ritual paintings relating to the occasion are made by a professionally trained painter. This painter is specially called for this occasion. These paintings decorating the walls all round include those of Ganeshaji, Riddhi-Siddhi, elephant riders (*gajaarohee*), horse riders (*ashvaarohee*), a security guard (*dwaarapaala*), etc. Along with these paintings we also notice paintings of some ladies lighting lamps (*diyaa*s), women holding fly-whisk (*chanvardhaarinee*), a water-woman (*panihaaree*), a lady with a mirror or a beautician (*darpanadharee* or *prasaadhikaa*), etc. All these paintings denote ritual ceremonies to be performed only and play important role in decorating the walls.

During the marriage ceremonies, elephants and

horses are very common and are being painted since time immemorial. They are given a special place in paintings on these occasions and have been considered a mark of respect. Elephant signifies power, progress and prosperity, while Lord Ganeshji is the symbol of auspiciousness and sacredness. A man riding a horse and sending a message, as depicted, is considered very auspicious. The paintings of the two parents-in-law arguing in a jovial mood are also drawn to add humour. These paintings remain there for several years even after the marriage ceremony is over reminding the coming generations of an auspicious occasion that has been solemnized here.

These paintings that are done in the wedding houses are also called the *chauk pooranaa* or *dhooli chitran* meaning painting the floor of a house for an auspicious occasion. On every festive occasion, these paintings are common. But slowly they regained their own importance and prominence for the solemn marriage rituals also. These paintings used to be drawn with the help of fingers only. Here the geometric figures — lines, circles, triangles, dots, etc. played a key role and had their own importance. After these geometric figures are drawn, they are filled with various colours made of wheat flour, red powder (*gulaal*), various other colourful powders made of different woods, vermilion, turmeric, rice, pulses, etc.

Marriage Preparations

This ritual indicates the initial marriage preparations going on at both the bride's and the groom's places of residence. After an auspicious date is decided upon, the preparations for the marriage begin.

Storehouse

Storehouse is the most important place in the house. After it is throughly cleaned, the keys are given to the keeper in charge of this room. All the items of daily consumption kept in the store are under the charge of the storekeeper. Wheat, pulses and other materials of regular consumption are brought in advance in large quantities and kept in this room. The cleaning of the food articles continues from morning till evening by the old ladies in the family. They do this with lots of enthusiasm amidst humming of ritual songs.

Utensils

All the utensils that are kept in the store are washed, cleaned and dried. As per the requirement, other utensils are also purchased.

Tailor

All the dresses of the gods and goddesses that are worshipped in the houses are stitched by the family tailor only. The tailor sits in the marriage house on all these occasions and works throughout day and night to complete the work in time.

Inviting Ganeshji (Ganeshji ko Nyontanaa)

Without the worship of Lord Ganeshji, no new work can begin, according to Hindu belief. Therefore, on the auspicious occasion of the marriage ceremony, the Lord is given the first invitation. The most auspicious amongst the gods, he is first requested and invited along with his consorts Riddhi and Siddhi to kindly grace the occasion with his esteemed presence and shower blessings on the newly married couple.

In Hindu rituals, worship of Ganeshji is very essential to begin any new work. It gives the work safety, stability and success. This ritual was prevalent in ancient days and it is continued till today successfully. As per the custom that is prevalent, after the date of marriage has been announced, the ladies in a group visit a Ganeshji temple in the village singing devotional songs in the Lord's praise. At the temple, the ladies offer sweets, ghee, and flowers and request the Lord to kindly grace the occasion along with his consorts Riddhi and Siddhi and bless the couple. In Rajasthan, there is a significant Ranthambhor Ganeshji. This is the reason why in many of the Ganeshji songs, the mention of Ranthambhor finds prominence. *Ranthambhor soom aayo re vinaayak.* In Mewar, invitation is given to Gogunda Ganeshji — *aaj mhaare gogundaa raa gunapat nootiyaa*. In Udaipur, Bohraa Ganeshji is given invitation. Similarly, in every district and in every state, a special invitation is given to Ganeshji for his gracious presence along with consorts Riddhi and Siddhi on the auspicious occasion. The women pick-up some soil or a stone from the temple precincts assuming it to be the Lord's blessings and take it along with them in a procession to their house and venerate it. At the house, a feast is organized for all the guests present. Earlier, the Lord is requested for his gracious presence along with both his consorts and shower his blessings. He is presented with vermilion and a book containing the invitation message which reads thus:

> सिद्धश्री विनायक जी, शुभ ओपमालयक श्रीमान् गणेशजी, लाभ–शुभ, रिद्धि–सिद्धि महारानी और समस्त मंगल परिवार सहित पधारसी।
>
> *siddhashree Vinaayakji, shubh opamaalayaka shreemaan Ganeshji, laabh-shubh, riddhi-siddhi mahaaranee aur samast mangal parivaar sahit padhaarasee*!
>
> O! Ganeshji, the one endowed with supernatural powers, the one who has no lord over him, the one wearing beautiful garlands, please come with your companions *laabh* (profit) and *shubh* (prosperity) and your queens Riddhi (good fortune) and Siddhi (accomplishment) along with all your auspicious family members to bless us.

After the invitation is given to Lord Ganeshji, invitation is sent individually to the houses of a painter, a whitewasher, a draper, a goldsmith, a potter, and many others. Everybody is humbly requested, with folded hands, to kindly make the occasion successful with their kind presence and good work.

Wedding Dates (Lagna Lekhan)

In this ceremony the family of the bride sends the horoscope to the groom's family so that the latter can show both the horoscopes to their family priests and select an auspicious and convenient date for the marriage. Simultaneously, dates for the other rituals, like seating ceremony (*paat bithaayee*), *yagya* for the peace in the household, etc. are decided upon. According to these auspicious dates only, the wedding invitation cards are printed.

Before the wedding invitation cards are printed, after invoking the blessings of Ganeshji a card is written and addressed to the family deity and sent to his temple or placed before the deity in the *poojaa* room of the house. Later in the bride's house there is a ritual of writing the auspicious time (*lagna*) for the marriage. The family priest or the family barber is called and asked to give the names of the groom's family elders and important guests. At that time the auspious date for the marriage, day, star, time (night) are written on a *lagna–patrikaa* (wedding card). In the earlier times also such card writing rituals were practised with equal mirth and gaiety. The card was called *madhuraakshar*. The mention of this is found in the *Valmiki Ramayana*'s Balakanda when the family members of Lord Raam, from the groom's side, are invited with humble and sweet words from the side of the bride Seetaa and requested to be present accompanied by musicians, elephants and horses at the appointed date and time and accept the hand of the bride for their groom (*paanigrahan*). The wedding card is sprinkled with vermilion, and full grains of rice dipped in turmeric are stuck on it. It is bound by a sacred red thread. The priest or barber from the side of the bride is asked to deliver these cards to the groom's house.

On the other hand, from the groom's side, a small ceremony is held when the marriage invitation is received from the bride's side. This ritual is called the invitation receiving ceremony. If there is no delay in the solemnization of marriage, the card is kept in the small temple in the house along with the picture of Shri Vinaayakji. And if there is still some time left for the ceremony, the booklet (card) is placed in a local temple near the house. At the time of departure of the marriage party, this booklet is taken along. While returning the next day, accompanied by the bride, this card is buried in a pit somewhere on the way home. It is this very card or booklet which, with the passage of time, became known as the *kumkum-patrikaa* or the vermilion card.

॥ *Shri Ganeshaay Namah* ॥

मनुहार पत्रिका

Invitational Request

Shri . . . .

With the blessings of the Almighty, the marriage ceremony of immortal Ganesh and the ever fortunate Riddhi-Siddhi has been decided to be solemnized on Friday, 12 December 2008 itself. The various programmes associated with the marriage will begin from Thursday, 11 December 2008. It is the close relatives and friends who make the atmosphere in a house cheerful, merry and lively. We crave your indulgence and send this prior information in the hope that you will kindly make it convenient to grace the occasion, by being present with all your family members, and honour us. The marriage invitation card giving the timings for the various ceremonies, will be sent to you soon.

But, if for some reason, the invitation does not reach you in time, we humbly request that you kindly consider this card itself as an invitation and be present on the auspicious occasion. Eagerly awaiting your arrival with your family.

Paarvatee and Shiva Shankar

॥ *Shri Ganeshaay Namah* ॥

Marriage Invitation

On the auspicious occasion of the marriage of

Chi. Ganesh
(Son of Paarvati and Shiva Shankar)

with

Sou. Kan. Riddhi-Siddhi
(Daughter of Vishvaroopa Prajaapati)

you are cordially invited to attend with your family.

RSVP
Kaartikeya

Vineet
Paarvati and Shiva Shankar

****

Wedding Programme

Sree Ganapati installation
Saturday, the 6th of December 2008
9 a.m.

Maayaraa
Thursday, the 11th of December 2008
11 a.m.

Departure of Baaraat
Friday, the 12th of December 2008, 5 p.m.

Paanigrahan
Friday, 12th December 2008, 11 p.m.

Sweet-making and Paddy Husking Ritual (Haath Dhaan)

This ritual means that at both the houses of the bride and the groom, celebrations are going on with full fervour and gaiety.

This ritual is performed on any proper time (*shubh muhurt*). In common parlance it is called the junior Vinaayakji ritual or even *chhotaa baan*. On the first day of the Vinaayakji, both the bride and the groom are given in their hands the *peethee* paste which is made of soaked and ground pulses (*daal*). Early in the morning, before the day break, when the sun is about to rise (*brahma-velaa*), at both the places of the bride and the groom, a group of ladies are seen preparing for the very first oil anointing ceremony. With ritual songs on their lips, they are in full gaiety to anoint the bride and the groom with oil and turmeric paste at their respective places of residence. In this ceremony, the whole body of the bride and groom is anointed with turmeric powder mixed with oil amidst the singing of traditions songs. The paste is put from head to toe and rubbed across the whole body. The ladies who perform this both ritual and change the bride's clothes are called *goranee*. They are usually five, seven or eleven in number. After the oil and turmeric paste anointing is over, it is time to give them bath and attire them in new clothes. After the bride and the groom have changed their clothes, begins the Ganapati *poojaa* (veneration) and *aarati.* A small child (male or female) is asked to sit near the bride and the groom. The child is considered the image of Vinaayakji and called *Vinaayakadaa.* After this, on a plate Ganapati *poojaa, kalash* (pitcher) *poojaa,* Lord Varun *poojaa,* Matrikaa (seven Devis) *poojaa* and Navgrah *poojaa* are done by the family priest. Ganeshji is adorned on the walls all around in the form of paintings and drawings. In the four corners and in the centre of the seat (*aasani*), five *svastikas* are drawn and a small Ganeshji, made of yellow mud, placed in the centre worshipped. The pitcher (*kalash*) is venerated, a lamp with ghee is lit and porridge made of flour, sugar and liquid is offered to the Lord. After the worship, sugar candies depicting the figures of gods-goddesses are distributed among all those present. The married sister or paternal aunt (*bhuaa*) performs *aartee* for the bride or the groom. The figures of hands made of *peethee* and henna (*mehandi*) paste are imprinted on both sides of Vinaayakji. Four married women accompany the bride or the groom to their respective seats. After the worshipping of Ganeshji is over, in a sacred pot some sweets, a little jaggery, pulses and a few coins are put and the mouth of this pot is covered with a red cloth and fastened tightly. Now, both the Vinaayakji and this pot are placed together and the Goddess of Wealth Lakshmiji's *poojaa aarati* is performed. The women who are assembled there, sing songs in praise of various gods-goddesses, till the whole *poojaa* is finished.

After completion of the sweet-taking ceremony, amidst the singing of songs, two women holding a winnow each sit on the floor, and four married women hold a big cloth of the size of a bed sheet over the heads of these two women — this ritual is called *chholdaaree.*

The two ladies then winnow salt, a rolling pin, coins, cotton balls, grass, turmeric sticks, jaggery, a bundle of thread and small quantities of seven grains put separately or together. This winnowing is done four times by each woman. After this the two other married women winnow grains. This ritual is called *haath dhaan* or *dhaan sohnaa.*

This day marks the end of all office and household chores for both the groom and the bride, and thus begins the auspicious work of marriage preparations. Sweets (*laddoo*s) made of gum and other material are given to them for eating. They are doted by family members till the marriage.

Establishing the Vinaayakji (Ganapati Sthaapanaa)

This ritual means establishing Ganeshji (Vinaayakji) at the appropriate place and direction in the house and setting up an auspicious space for performing the marriage rituals.

For marriage rituals or to start any new work, worship of Ganeshji is very important. No work can be done successfully without the worship of Ganeshji with proper rites and rituals. If this ritual is performed and Ganeshji is venerated with all rites, any work becomes very easy to perform, success is achieved and there will be enough storage of grains in the house. In several houses, five married women accompany the chief lady of the family to the popular Vinaayak temple adjoining their house, or in the adjoining villages or important cities. They extend invitation to Lord Ganeshji with his whole family to personally come and grace the occasion.

The ladies carry with them a steel plate containing Rs. 51 or Rs. 101 and sweets with a *svastika* sign made in the middle of the plate. The chief lady places a small statue of Ganeshji in the middle of the plate and adorns it with a red cloth. She places the idol of Ganeshji at the auspicious place of worship in the house. She then sends, as per rituals, gifts, sweets and fruits, along with a lump of jaggery, all kept in a large steel plate to the potter's wife in the village.

At the marriage house, Vinaayakji, i.e. Ganeshji, has been established at the most sacred place. On the freshly painted wall, a painting of Ganeshji is made. On the right and left of Ganeshji, his consorts Riddhi and Siddhi are shown whisking him. Near the feet of Ganeshji, his carriage, the mouse is placed. On the lower part of Ganeshji, seven small round marks with vermilion or ghee are made. Very near to the picture or painting, a pitcher is placed on whole wheat and maize seeds. Nearby a lamp is lit with ghee. This lamp will remain burning throughout day and night as long as it is in this place of worship as this auspicious place is where all marriage rituals and ceremonies will be held. This is called *kohabar* in some places while it is called *vardevaasaa* in other regions. This Ganesh installation is done in both the bride's and groom's houses.

This holy place is kept pure and clean till the end of the ceremony. No man or woman who is impure is allowed to enter this place. All the rituals of the bride and groom done at this spot are considered sacred.

Invitation has already been sent to Ganeshji in the adjoining temples in the village. After relations have been established between the bride and the groom, it is considered auspicious to invite the gods and goddesses and even our ancestors through proper rituals. This is part of our custom. The ceremony of marriage is begun with the ritual worship of Ganeshji as is common with all new ventures, by establishing in the house the Vighnahartaa (obstacle remover), Mangal-moorti (auspicious god), the Siddhi Vinaayak (the one without a lord over him and one who bestows all achievements). All the relatives, friends and neighbours take part in the ritual and shower their blessings. In fact, Shri Ganesh (inauguration) of all rituals, including marriages, begins only with the establishment of Siddhi Vinaayak in the house. Ganeshji is the Lord of obstacles and relieves us of all sins and difficulties. Therefore, it is hoped that the auspicious occasion should go on without any hindrance. Ganeshji sees it all with his sharp eyes and hears it all, with his big ears and after grasping all news he keeps them in his big belly, so that no news is leaked out and no trouble is started. He is prayed to shower on us that knowledge to overcome all problems and to face them boldly and wisely. After the ceremony has begun, the fathers of bride and groom invite their ancestors with full rites and rituals and take their blessings. Where the food, grains and other items are stored, the God of Food is worshipped so that the food store should be full. Here, the goddess of food is Prithvi (earth) and the Lord of food is Vishnu, and both are venerated on this occasion.

It is to be noted that after the completion of five or seven days of the ceremony of the junior Vinaayak, a large-sized Vinaayak is established at its place amongst celebrations, with fervour and gaiety. In the morning, the bride and the groom are anointed with oil.

Applying Perfumed Paste (Haldi-Chandan)

This ritual is to apply the perfumed paste (*Ubatan*) made up of sandalwood powder, wheat flour, turmeric powder, oils and various perfumes on the bodies of both the bride and the groom before taking bath. The paste softens and glows the skin.

This ritual starts about three to five days before marriage in a city or town or when the bride and groom arrive at their relatives' houses in a village near to the place of marriage. These relatives and friends together enjoy and take part in the morning and evening feasts, besides involving in other day-to-day social functions that are being celebrated in the house. These functions happen separately at both the houses of bride and the groom. As per the auspicious time, bride and groom are seated on the "throne" or wooden seats. On this occasion all the ladies wear yellow dresses. The seat's four legs are tied with untwisted red-coloured thread and the bride and groom sit on them facing east. After this ritual both the bride and groom are not supposed to step out of their houses and are in the company of their brothers, sisters-in-law and friends. Due to unforeseen circumstances if they have to go out of the houses they have to carry a small packet or bundle of yellow mustard or a small knife.

Then a paste is made of soaked *daal* (*peethee*) that includes barley flour, turmeric powder, almonds, *chironjee* (a kind of dry fruit), perfumed oil or *ghee*, etc. Nowadays, people prefer to use the readymade pastes. This paste is rubbed four times on the whole body of the bride and the groom. It is usually done by the sisters-in-law, or the paternal aunts (*chaachee*s) or even sometimes by the brother's wife (*bhaabhi*). There are usually five married women who perform this ritual. One by one they come and apply the paste four times each, from toes to head, then the shoulders, the back, the feet, the knees, and the feet on all sides. This is followed by the ritual of husking the grains. Two women are seen, holding the winnowing basket, and sitting facing each other. The basket contains seven different kinds of grains and a rolling pin. The two women exchange these grains into each other's basket without allowing even a single piece of grain fall on the ground. On culmination of this ritual, all the elders, relatives and friends present on the occasion adorn the bride or the groom, by putting a small mark on their forehead (*teekaa*) and shower blessings on them. The bride or the groom accepts their blessings by reverentially bowing down before them and touching their feet. Gifts are presented to both the bride and the groom by them. The ladies of the house sing ritual songs on this occasion. The songs include all the actions and emotions involved in going through the ceremonies and performing this ritual. It demands and involves all the young and the old alike, as the occasion demands, and their enjoyment and gaiety is very well known.

After this, a male barber takes the groom; and a lady from the beauty parlour takes the bride to a separate room. They massage each of them with a slightly tough hand so that their whole body glows and shines. The turmeric paste is used not only for glowing the skin but it also acts as an antiseptic cream. It is believed that by using the turmeric paste mixed with oils and perfumes, the bodies of both the bride and the groom glow. There is a shine on their face, besides it makes the body soft, smooth and beautiful. With red and green-coloured bangles on the bride's hands, and with turmeric paste applied on the whole face and body, the bride looks extra soft and graceful.

The couple have different looks altogether. Use of turmeric paste on this occasion also means that the bride has been "booked" for marriage, as it is also used in a Hindi proverb — *haath peele karnaa*, especially for the brides. There is also a belief that people on the side of bride feel that till yesterday their daughter was an ordinary girl, but from today she will be a bride, a *grihlakshmi* (wealth of the house). She will have to take some very tough decisions and own up responsibilities from now onwards, and which she had never faced in her life till now. A new responsibility will have to be shouldered by her by entering into a new family. Therefore, this turmeric paste has been applied to make her hands tough so that she is to fulfil the job successfully.

Tying of Safety Thread (Dolda Baandhanaa)

This ritual is performed to identify the bride and the groom separately and to sing songs for their safety. This ritual consists of a red silken thread, a twine or a bundle of threads that are wound and made into a thick thread (like bracelet). A small sea shell, an iron ring, and a wax seal are tied in a small red cloth bag containing a little salt and mustard seeds. This thread is tied on the right hand and the right foot of the groom, while it is tied on the left hand and left foot of the bride. From this day onwards, both the bride and the groom are forbidden to eat sour and hot foods. The singing of ritual songs of marriage begins and continues till the ceremony of marriage is over. It is believed that by performing this ritual, both the bride and groom are protected from all sorts of bad luck or mishaps.

During this ceremony in their respective houses, both the parents of the bride and the groom are present. On this very day the Saankadee Vinaayak is also established. Lord Saankadee is seen in the form of a bangle or anklet and denotes the ritual of the sacred thread which is tied on the hands and the feet of the couple to be married. This thread is tied in knots which range from one to 100 and may be even more. These knots signify the kaarmic bonds between the bride and groom. After the marriage ceremony is over, both the bride and the groom together involve themselves in untying these knots, to the merriment of those present. Sometimes, the friends of the bride apply cactus juice or liquid on the knots and this makes the knots sticky and strong and the groom finds it very difficult to untie the knots. The ritual also means that the relation between the bride and the groom, should be firm, strong, and bound in togetherness as these knots, which cannot be easily separated.

Wedding Cards Distribution Ceremony (Battisee)

This ritual called *battisee jhelaanaa* denotes the delivery of the wedding invitation cards to the maternal grandparents of the couple. The mothers of both the bride and the groom go to their respective parents' houses to deliver the wedding cards. This ceremony is performed at both the houses of the bride and the groom separately. The mother gives the invitation of marriage to her brother, mother and father along with all the near and dear relatives.

The sister (i.e. mother of the bride or the groom) goes to her brother's house taking with her a large steel plate containing 32 numbers of several items. Hence the name of the ritual. These items include 32 *mohar* or pieces of gold or 32 silver coins, some cash, 32 betel nuts, a coconut, turban and dresses for her brother and sister-in-law. She requests her brother to grace the marriage ceremony accompanied by her sister-in-law (*bhaabhi*) and all other family members. The sister brings with her porridge (*lapsee*) and distributes it amongst all her relatives and family members along with the wedding invitation. This *lapsee* distribution ritual indicates that the wedding cards distribution ceremony is over.

This ceremony is followed by the ritual of

worshipping the musical instruments — drums like the *nagaadaa, dhol,* etc. and later also venerating the big sized pan (*kadhaaee*) and other utensils in which all the dishes for the marriage ceremony are to be prepared. All this is done in a very ritualistic way.

Worshipping of Musical Instruments — Nagaadaa and Dhol

Five days before the auspicious ceremony of marriage, a large-sized drum (*nagaadaa*) is established at the main entrance gate. But before this, the verandah and all the open spaces in front of the house are washed and cleaned thoroughly. The royal astrologer gives a helping hand and takes utmost care in decorating the house and the open spaces. The drum is placed at the entrance with all respects and worshipped. A *svastik* mark is put in the middle of the drum and covered with a red cloth and a little jaggery is kept on it. The ritual songs in praise of gods and goddesses are sung to seek their blessings. These rituals and *poojaa*s are performed everyday amidst music, dance, fun and frolic till the marriage is finally over and the ladies of the family sing songs of praise worshipping the drums and other musical instruments.

Worshipping Pans and Other Utensils

About four to five days before the marriage ceremony, the preparation of sweets begins. The royal cook or chief cook is summoned by the family and the making of sweets begin. This is done only after the ritual worship and veneration of the various utensils brought into use for making sweets have been completed. The main big utensil (*kadhaaee*) is venerated by covering it with a red cloth. Some grains of rice are sprinkled over it and vermilion (*kumkum*) is applied; jaggery is kept over it and hymns recited. It is then respectfully placed in the kitchen. First the sweet liquid (*lapsee*) is made and offered to all the gods and goddesses in the house — Vinaayakji and others — and their blessings are sought. This is later distributed among all the members of the family present. Normally two kitchens are established — one for making vegetarian food only, while the other for non-vegetarian food. Everyday the sweet liquid (*lapsee*) is made in the morning as a first dish. It is then kept before the gods and goddesses and their blessings sought. Only after this, the preparation for any other food begins. After establishing the Lord Vinaayak in the house, *kadhee* is not made. [*Kadhee* means a curry made out of sour liquid (*dahee*).]

Ritual of Inviting the Royal Family

A separate invitation is sent to the king, the queen and other members of the royalty. The mother of the bride or the groom, accompanied by four other senior ladies and three elderly gentlemen, wearing their traditional dresses, considered a ritual, enter the royal palace. They all bow before the royal family. Along with the invitation cards, they bring a large silver plate containing lumps of jaggery covered with a red cloth.

Henna Ritual (Mehandi Rachaav)

This ceremony is considered very sacred and is said to bring good fortune before and after marriage.

Henna signifies prosperity in life. Our culture mentions henna as a cosmetic item and also a sign of prosperity. The other quality that is mentioned is that it gives peace and coolness to the mind and body when applied. Any work that is performed peacefully and with cool mind gives double enjoyment. It is said that henna when applied on the hands has its direct effect on the heart.

When there is a marriage, there must definitely be the henna ceremony. During the marriage ceremonies, the henna is applied on both the hands and feet of the bride. All married ladies present in the house, whether she is a daughter or a daughter-in-law or sister-in-law, applies henna. Gum and tea leaves soaked in water are mixed with henna powder. This is done so that it becomes a paste and gains a darker colour. After it is prepared, it is applied with a very thin and fine tipped stick or put in a plastic cone with a hole at the tip and then applied on the hands. This henna ceremony goes on till the marriage day. It is a ritual in Hindu society particularly in Rajasthan, that whenever a married woman goes to her parents' house from her in-laws' house, or vice versa, she adorns the colour of henna on her hands. Today, we find that even the bridegrooms are seen applying henna on their hands and this has even become a ritual in some castes.

The atmosphere all around during this ceremony is full of laughter, joy and gaiety. The bride's friends, sisters-in-law and the neighbourhood girls are seen frolicking and making fun on the private life of the bride and the groom.

Henna is usually applied in two ways — one is the drawing of lines while the other is by putting on dots. During the marriage ceremonies, usually the henna is applied by making the shapes of betel leaves, a lotus, oleander flowers, etc. The henna is usually applied in the traditional ways — five dots design, betel leaf design, straight lines design or waves-like design. During the celebration of this ritual, various henna songs are sung which makes the whole atmosphere cheerful and merry. Some of the wordings of these songs go like this:

> भंवर पूंचो छोड़ोजी हाथां पे रच रही मेहंदी . . . मेहंदी तो वाई मालवे जी को रंग गयो गुजरात रे मेहंदी रंग लागो . . . ।
>
> *bhamvar pooncho chhodojee haathaan pe rach rahee mehandi . . . mehandi to vaayee maalave jee ko rang gayo gujaraat re mehandi rang laago . . .* ।

After the completion of this henna ceremony, the ladies who helped in putting on henna are suitably rewarded in cash and kind.

Taking out Small Wedding Procession (Bindaulaa) Ceremony in Localities

After establishing the idol of Vinaayakji in the marriage house, the very first invitation to both the bride or the groom for a feast comes from their very close relatives (as this ritual is practised in both houses separately). On this day, all the members that are present in the house of the bride or the groom, together go in a procession with full pomp and show to the relatives' house. This ritual helps in the introduction between the relatives amongst themselves. The sumptuous food consists of sweets, fruits and several other salty dishes. After the food is over, the friends and relatives who participated in the feast are given farewell by applying *tilak* (mark on their forehead) and given a token amount in cash which may be a rupee or a bigger amount depending upon the individual's status. Gifts are also given along with a coconut. This formality is called the *bindaulaa* giving ceremony. This ceremony also helps in understanding each and every relative very closely, and personally and having closer intimacy with each other. From the house to which the first *bindaulaa* procession goes, at the time of dusk, the procession is given farewell with full respect, accompanied by music and dance, till they returned to the bride or the groom's house. Special songs for the purpose are also sung. Therefore, through this ceremony the bride or the groom is first introduced to the relatives and their neighbours. People, not only from the bride or groom's side enjoy this ceremony, but their neighbours also enjoy very much. Thus, this ceremony signifies one of the famous social customs that prevail in our society.

Establishing the Sacred Pitcher (Kalash Sthaapanaa)

This ritual means going to a potter's house and bringing a pitcher to be established in the marriage house.

After the idol of Vinaayakji has been established in the house, on the eve of marriage, in both the bride and the groom's houses, a pitcher is brought and established. This pitcher is brought in a procession with fun and frolic, and is accompanied by loud music and a group of ladies who sing ritual songs for the occasion. It is a belief that as a potter moulds the mud, smoothens it and then shapes it into beautiful pots, similarly the new bride and groom should understand their married life and help each other to give it a proper shape for progress and development. On reaching the potter's house, first a ritual to worship the potter's wheel is performed. The pot made with this wheel is worshipped with proper rituals, with the help of vermilion (*roli*), rice grains, red thread (*mauli*), etc. In fact, with the development of wheel began the progress of society. It brought prosperity all over and many items of everyday use were made with clay. This credit only goes to the potter who is, therefore, given a special place in a marriage house. The potter's wife is given a shawl that is put around her neck and shoulders. The potter is given a *siropaava* (cloth of honour). The accompanying ladies request the potter's wife to prepare a few pots for them. The ladies have already given the potter the wedding invitation earlier. The potter gives some pots to the ladies who put a *tilak* (mark) on these pots with vermilion (*kumkum*) and gracefully accept them. A silver or golden belt (*karadhanee*) is put around the pot, a thick ring made of cloth (*idonee*) to balance the pots is kept on the head and the pots balanced carefully one above the other. Forming a long queue, the women return carrying pitchers on their heads, dancing and frolicking all the way home. During marriage ceremonies, about five, seven or eleven pots are required. These pots are usually brought by the ladies who may include mother, elder daughter-in-law, the youngest daughter-in-law, sisters, paternal aunt, etc. The procession is usually led by the mother of the bride or the groom. At some places, even the ladies from the potter's family help in carrying the pitchers, and lead the procession. This custom varies from place to place. These ladies carry and display these beautiful pitchers all the way with pleasure and place them at the Vinaayak's (auspicious) place in the marriage house. There are several songs that are popular on this occasion. This ritual is also called the *baasan* (vessel) ritual. When the ladies carrying the pitchers reach home, they are helped by the son-in-law in putting them at the auspicious place. For this he is given a token gift or cash.

Waking up the Whole Night (The Raatijagaa)

This ceremony is performed for the welfare of both the bride and the groom.

On the appointed day, the family gods and goddesses are worshipped the whole night amid the sounds of music, drums and other instruments. In royal families, this ritual is perfomed in the temple of Baana Maataa. A ghee lamp will burn the whole night before the idols of the gods-goddesses. After the completion of this ceremony, henna is soaked and all present on the occasion apply it on their hands. Blessings are sought from all the gods-goddesses and even ancestors, who are revered on this day.

Raatijogaa implies waking up the whole night to sing songs in praise of the gods-goddesses. They are requested to bless the couple by their gracious presence on the auspicious occasion for their long life, good health and prosperity. Amongst these songs, the most popular ones are about the various gods-goddesses, Sati Maataa and songs requesting the ancestors to kindly shower their blessings. There are so many songs that one gets engrossed in singing them. When the night has passed into the dawn, one never comes to know of it, as everyone is so engrossed in the enchanting songs. This ritual is simultaneously performed in the groom's house on the marriage day, before the departure of (*baaraat*) marriage procession and in the bride's house, a day before the marriage or on the wedding night.

As a ritual, the bride is applied henna. This ritual signifies peace, progress and prosperity and helps to destroy all evils that may have come in the bride's or the groom's lives till then and that both should work for the welfare of people and lead a happy life. These blessings are attained from various gods-goddesses and also from the ancestors who are recalled and praised in the form of songs.

Taking out Wedding Procession (The Bindaulee)

This ritual means taking out again a small wedding procession (called the *bindaulee*) of the groom through the market consisting of only male friends and relatives.

In royal families, only the *bindaulee* of a groom is taken out which consists of only male members. The groom rides on a horseback and is taken out of the palace for a short distance and brought back to the palace. Nowadays it has become a custom to take out marriage processions from both the bride and the groom's houses. Both the bride and the groom are given a small iron knife or a dagger to keep with them. They are now forbidden to wander outside the house. In the evening, the first *bindaulee* is organized and taken out to a brahman's house. At the groom's place and also at his *guru*'s or at the family priest's place on this occasion, special auspicious rice is prepared. After this the *bindaulee* procession is taken out through the market amidst music and dance. In several castes, it is prevalent that the bride's *bindaulee* is taken out, with a covering over her head. This covering of cloth is held by four women. The *bindaulee* of the groom is taken out with him riding on horseback. Often a small child, in the form of a Vinaayakji, sits with the groom on horseback. Bride's is taken out sometimes in an open buggy or a carriage. Along with the bride, often her friends and small children (as Vinaayak's form) also sit in the carriage. Following this procession are several women, and girls of the marriage family, singing ritual songs. Today, we see ladies, gentlemen, friends and relatives of the groom dancing merrily all along the procession route to the accompaniment of band music.

Song and Dance Assembly
(Geet-sangeet Mahfil)

This ritual is full of songs, music, dance, laughter and merry making.

It is very common that songs are sung everyday in marriage houses. According to the ancient custom, the singing of marriage songs begins 11 or 21 days before the date of marriage ceremony. But today, we have a very limited time for everything and hence a very short programme of music is followed. There are different songs that are sung in the evening and the morning hours. During evening song (*sandhyaa geet*) celebrations, an iron lamp is lit and placed near the entrance to the bride or groom's house. There ladies sing various ritual songs, including the popular songs in praise of various gods and goddesses. A married woman starts the session by singing the first line of a song, and all the others continue the songs. The widows do not sing any song. The songs cover the marriage tales of Shiva-Paarvati, Raam-Seetaa, Shri Krishna-Rukmini, etc. This marriage song ritual is also called Byaavalaa." Many times riddles are also being asked during these ceremonies. In Rajasthan, these riddles are also called "Paarasiyaan." The women who attend this ceremony are given gifts, sweets and cash when they leave.

In the royal families, it is customary that these

songs, music, dance, etc. start in the evening of the day the oil anointing ceremony begins. Usually the songs are sung in two different groups — ladies and gentlemen separately. The ladies usually assemble on the verandah. A red sheet is spread and cushions and pillows are kept along with wooden low chairs. Special arrangements are made for the bride to sit. On this day, the bride is in a very simple make-up and attired in light coloured new dresses. She wears a necklace and a flower bracelet on her hands. In the beginning, the professional lady singers who are called for the occasion, sing songs praising the family goddesses. Later other family ladies join them in music and dance. All the guests present shower money on the singers which are later shared by the singers, the helpers and other workers.

When the queen from the royal family expresses her desire to dance, the king is requested to be present there. When he arrives all the people get up and stand and honour him. The king is seated on a special royal seat. He remains there for a few minutes, showers money on the queen, distributes cash and gifts to the singers and goes back to his chamber. The singers stand all the time and sing when the royalty is present. The relatives of both the bride and the groom and near relatives are invited on this occasion and given gifts before they leave. The bride and the groom are even given cash by these relatives.

With the passage of time, these rituals are reduced due to the shortage of time. On one particular day, all these ceremonies are held together. Sometimes famous professional male or female singers are invited for the occasion. Food and drinks are also served. This ceremony is known as the *mahilaa sangeet* (or ladies *sangeet*). Nowadays this function has become very popular and is generally done a day before the marriage.

Worshipping the Earth (Rodee Poojan)

This ritual is to worship the earth and seek blessings of patience and tolerance from Mother Earth.

The day after "Raatijagaa" (waking up the whole night), or on the day of marriage, this ritual is perfomed early in the morning. At some places, this ceremony is performed on the day Vinaayakji has been established. This ceremony is performed by women only. This ritual is also called the *ghooraapoojan* (worshipping the dungheap). In fact, this is a ritual of worshipping the mother earth only. In the songs that are sung during this ritual, *rodee* or stones are compared to diamonds. It is the earth alone which is taking on all the weight upon it with so much patience and tolerance, and multiplying our happiness manifold.

The groom goes out of the house early in the morning. Under cover of the veil of a married women, he is taken near the garbage dump for performing this ceremony. A thin iron rod pierced through a small wheel (*taaklaa*) is fixed into the ground by the groom and then begins the veneration ceremony. A barber's wife holds the plate containing *poojaa* materials which include *kumkum* (vermilion), rice grains, *mauli* (red thread), betel nuts and some flowers. After doing *poojaa* to the *taaklaa* all the people return to the house.

Then the barber's wife removes the iron rod from the dump along with a little earth. The soil attached to the *taaklaa* is kept in the grain store in the house on the day of the big feast. It is believed that by performing this ritual, there will never occur any shortage of grains and the store will always remain full. There will also be no hurdle in the marriage proceedings and there will be wealth and prosperity in the household at all times.

The earth worship signifies that as the earth bears on its surface the wind, the rain, the sun, etc. with utter tolerance, similarly the bride and the groom should also show extreme coolness and patience in their lives. As the garbage collects all the waste items at one place without any distinction, in the same way the new couple should never distinguish between relatives and consider all of them as their own and live amicably.

Maternal House's Gift (Maayara)

This ritual means bringing gifts from the family of the maternal grandfather for both the bride and the groom and all the other relatives. These gifts are given to the bride a day before the marriage and to the bridegroom before the *baaraat* leaves the house.

The maternal uncles or mother's close relatives perform this ceremony by bringing a dress for the bride and the groom along with other gifts for all family members. The ritual is to bring closeness and better understanding amongst all the relatives and facilitates introduction among themselves. This ritual is also called the *mamera*, i.e. from maternal side. It is commonly understood that the maternal household bears half the expenditure of marriage, i.e. if it is economically strong and well off. The relatives from the maternal side perform this ritual very enthusiastically with open heart and bring the gifts beautifully wrapped for all relatives with great interest.

The relatives present at the groom's or bride's place welcome and accept the gifts respectfully and there is an atmosphere of enthusiasm, fun and gaiety all around. Various ritual songs are sung on this occasion. From the maternal house, gifts (and clothes) for all — mother, father, the bride, the groom, all relatives present, even for the ancestors, the gods and the goddesses are also brought on the occasion. The maternal uncle (*maamaa*) honours his brother-in-law and applies *tilak* on the forehead of each member of his sister's husband's family. He also hands over gifts, cash and ornaments to his sister. The brother is honoured and a *tilak* is applied on his forehead. He embraces his sister and wishes for her welfare and well-being. All members from the in-law's house are served cold drinks and snacks. The songs that are sung on this occasion are simple but meaningful and clearly contain brotherly love and emotions like —

> कणी रे दसा में उड़े रे गुलालां . . . ।
> कठै सूं आई सूंठ कठै सूं आयो जीरो,
> कठै सूं आयो ए गौरी भावज थारो बीरो . . . ।
>
> *kanee re dasaa mein ude re gulaalaan . . .*
> *kathai soon aayee soonth kathai soon aayo jeero,*
> *kathai soon aayo ye gauree bhaavaj thaaro beero . . .* ।

This ritual is a very emotional one for both families, especially for the mothers of the bride and the groom. Their paternal relatives perform this ritual which consists of *siropaav*s (ceremonial robe) and cash for all brothers, sisters and close relatives accompanied by boxes of sweets and fruit baskets. The attendants are also given gifts and turbans. First, the parents of both bride and the groom are asked to stand near the maternal uncle (*maamaajee*). A *tilak* is applied by him on his sister's forehead and gifts are given. Later, he honours his brother-in-law. The sister puts some money over his brother's head and gives her blessings. This money is picked up by the helpers and distributed amongst themselves. Even they shower on him their blessings. The sister serves her brother rose syrup and pleases him. This ritual is performed by all his cousins from the maternal side who have come to grace the ceremony. The mother seeks blessings by touching the feet of all her elderly relatives present. After this she invites all the guests inside for snacks and refreshments. After the completion of this ceremony, the parents of the bride (and the groom) seek the blessings from their parents and all other elders present there.

Horse Worship and Departure of Baaraat (Nikaasi)

This ritual is to worship the horse and to formally depart for the bride's place in a procession, accompanied by music and band. This is done only at the groom's house.

The owner of the horse is invited on this occasion. Since the groom is considered on this day as a king, his procession is taken out making him ride on a horse. Near the groom are seen his attendants, one of them holding an umbrella, the other seen with a flywhisk moving it in a circular motion over the groom. The horse is fastened to a stake, and given grams to eat. The houseowner brings silver jewellery for adorning the horse. The face, neck and back of the horse are decorated with trinkets and red silk cloth.

Earlier, before the departure of the wedding procession the ritual of oil anointment and *peethee* ceremony of groom are held. After these ceremonies an unmarried girl brings plain curd in a small vessel along with a small rolling pin. She stirs the curd with the rolling pin and pours this on the groom's head. The groom goes and takes bath. The barber — (nowadays a servant) helps the groom in taking bath. A married woman (*Suvaasini*) is called to assist the groom in wearing his new clothes. The woman, in return, gets some cash as a token of thanks. After wearing new clothes, the head of the groom is adorned with a turban and feather of a peacock or a crest of gold or pearls is pinned to this turban. Groom is adorned with diamond and gold necklaces and strings of pearls. The jewellery's pomp and show represents the position of the king and the respect his royal family enjoys in his ruling state.

After wearing new clothes, the groom is given a mixture of six things — green gram, coriander leaves, betelnut and a coin kept in a ball of jaggery and bound by red-coloured thread. They are all kept in a green leafcup, called *donaa*. This cup is kept in the groom's hand by some ladies. The groom returns the green cup back to the ladies. This ritual can be done by both ladies or gentlemen. Ritual songs are also sung on this occasion.

After the completion of the worship of Vinaayakji, prayers are recited so that the ceremony goes on and finishes without any hitch or hindrance. All the male members pay obeisance to the elders of the family and seek their blessings. Then the mother of the groom brings a silver necklace. She touches this necklace to the chest of the groom, to the cord of a churning stick, to her nose ring and to her saree's veil. She does this seven times. The mother then covers her breast with a veil and allows the teats to touch his son's (the groom) lips, i.e. symbolically breast-feeds him. The implication of this ritual is to remind the groom that he should always respect the sanctity of his mother's liquid. The mother gives permission to the groom to proceed further and perform his next duty in life, i.e. to become a householder, and blesses him. She also gives a small amount of cash to his son as a token pocket money. All those present on this occasion also give cash and a coconut to the groom and bless him.

The groom's elder sister-in-law applies collyrium (*kaajal*) to the eyes of the groom. She first applies *kaajal* to one of his eyes and then waits to receive a cash token or gift from him. When satisfied, she puts it in his other eye also. Before the departure of the wedding procession (*baaraat*), the conveyance of the groom, a female horse (a mare), is worshipped. The ladies put *kaajal* to the horse's eyes, put a garland, apply henna and put a *tilak* (a mark) with *kumkum* or rice grains on its forehead. A yellow cloth is put around its neck and it is given soaked gram pulse with jaggery and sugar candies to eat. The mother then rubs the horse with her hands, gives him her blessings amidst the singing of ritual songs. These songs are known as *ghoree geet,* and are sung to wish for a safe journey to the bride's place and return with the bride in all glory.

As the groom is about to get up on the horse, the sisters catch hold of the reins of the horse and feed it with gram and jaggery. The sisters leave the reins only when they are given cash or gifts by the groom. After this, all the sisters dance to music in front of the horse. The procession then departs for the bride's place. This is called the *var nikaasee* ritual or depature of the wedding procession. On both the sides of the horse are seen attendants (barber in olden days) waving fly whisks. The man with scented water walks behind the horse and sprinkles it on the procession, and the ceremonial stick or staff-bearer walks in front. When the procession reaches about half a kilometre from the house, all the male members join the groom. The procession halts either at a relative's house or at any banquet hall where the arrangment for food has been made. The bridegroom does not return to his house until he brings the groom with him. All the people including the groom have their meals and continue the *baaraat* procession. In royal families, all the necessary items required, including refreshments, go along with the *baaraat* procession.

Songs of Congratulations (Badhaave ke Geet)

This ritual of singing songs of congratulations is performed by the women present in the groom's house with music immediately after the wedding procession has left for the bride's house. On the same day the *choodaa* ceremony (wearing wedding bangles) is also performed. In the house, the ladies anxiously wait for the wedding procession to return with the bride, and exchange congratulatory messages and sing ritual songs amongst themselves. These songs have their own relevance and are sung on all rituals that bring happiness, peace, prosperity and progress.

Fun, Frolic and Jokes (Toontiyaa)

After the *baaraat* has left for the bride's place, the women at the groom's place sing ritual songs and keep the atmosphere cheerful and happy. When the rituals of marriage and circumambulation around the sacred fire are being performed by the bride and the groom at the former's residence, the women at the groom's house are busy cracking jokes and jocularly teasing each other.

Some of the ladies are seen imitating the gentlemen's voice and mimicking them. Any one of the sisters or daughters acts the part of a groom and the other becomes a bride. They mimic and crack jokes making the whole atmosphere filled with fun, mirth and laughter all around. Without these rituals, the wedding ceremony becomes dull and dry. This ritual is still performed with great spirit in many villages even today. The ritual is performed for the reason that when all the gentlemen have left with the procession, only ladies are left behind in the house. To keep the ladies awake the whole night and to see that nobody goes to sleep, this fun-loving ritual is performed. But today, this ritual is not performed with much interest and enthusiasm.

This uncommon ritual in Rajasthan is given the name *toontiyaa* or *khodiyaa* and in Bundelkhand it is popularly called *nakataa naach.* This is a witty ritual of marriage and all characters participating in this ritual are females only. It is said that when Lord Krishna's marriage procession proceeded for his bride's place, the ladies who stayed behind sang these ritual songs to keep them awake the whole night. Later this ritual became an important part in marriages.

Pillar-erecting Ceremony (Thaam/Maandaa Ropanaa)

This ritual is performed on the occasion of marriage by installing a pillar or a post in the house.

Inside the marriage place — banquet or open place, in one corner, a small stage is set and a pillar is installed. The Brahman priest installs this post in the presence of the bride only.

In fact, on all important occasions this pillar-erecting ceremony is performed. All the important functions are performed around this post and it signifies the symbol of stability. This ritual was usually performed in the royal houses by the royal family priests only. But nowadays, this ritual is performed by the bride's paternal uncle or her brother-in-law.

The pillar represents the sacred sacrificial hall or *yagya mandap*. The pillar is made of a new bamboo. On the upper part of it is attached a circular wooden plate having four hooks. The hooks and the plates are attached with small sticks and a frame is formed. On this plate or frame some mud is kept and a pot is placed over it. On the mouth of the pot a coconut is kept. Before installing this post, one has to dig a one-foot deep pit. In cities, a big tin box or drum is used instead. In this box, green gram, some flowers, water, sugar candies, etc.

are put and the pillar is made to stand in it. In front of this post are placed two small wooden stools on which are drawn the figures of 16 *maatrikaa*s and the nine planets. On one side of the stage is kept a pot, while a lamp is kept on the other side. On this occasion, ritual songs are also sung and the post is worshipped. In this ceremony, sometimes the parents of the bride also take part. This ceremony is solemnized at the bride's house early in the morning on the wedding day. It is only after this the other ceremonies take place.

During this pillar-erecting ceremony, various gods like the Earth, the Varaah (the boar *avataar* of Vishnu) and the Sheshnaag (the serpent bed of Vishnu) are worshipped. The post is also worshipped at its lower portion as Lord Brahma, the middle as Lord Vishnu and the top of the post, near the pot, as Lord Shiva. Ritual songs are also sung by the ladies on this occasion. The parents of the bride keep fast on this day and take a vow and pray to the post for the welfare and prosperity of their daughter. After the culmination of this ceremony, the following *mantra* is recited —

धरणीधरशास्त्रिकृतो वैवाहिक-स्तम्भरोपण सरलविधिः सम्पूर्णः ।

dharaneedhara shaastrikrito vaivaahik-stambharopan saralavidhih sampoornah

Setting up a Marriage Platform (Lagna Mandap)

A platform is set for the marriage rituals to be performed by the family.

Usually, the marriage ritual is performed at the bride's place of residence only. The whole house is decorated with flowers, lights and auspicious signs.

For performing the marriage rituals these temporary platforms are erected. These are usually made in the middle of the ground or a place where the marriage takes place. The place is smeared with cowdung paste and purified. Small earthen pots numbering nine or eleven are kept one above the other giving it a pillar shape and tied to the four corners of the stage with saffron thread. These empty pots are tied with saffron thread and coloured in red. These pots are kept safely in the house for about a year and later immersed in flowing waters of the river. These pots are brought by the local potter couple, who are honoured with a shawl, a turban, a lump of jaggery, grains and cash. Nowadays, these earthen pots have been replaced by other material. The stage is decorated with fragrant flowers on all sides, mud pots, incenses, perfumes and colourful strips of cloth. The stage is further beautified by using red colour (*gulaal*), turmeric powder and also wheat flour. On the stage, the four directions are established as *agni-kon* in the south-east direction — the *maatrikaa mandal; ishaan-kon* in the north-east direction — the *navagraha mandal;* in the southern direction the Brahma; and in the northern direction the *praneetaa prokshanee* (finger-ring made of *kusha* grass) is established. This is made of *doorba* grass in different combinations and bound with red coloured thread, and is also called *upanayan kushaa.*

On all four corners of this stage, wooden pegs are fixed to the ground and a red thread tied round them. Sometimes the strings are also covered with barley. The first peg is facing the pillar. On all the four pegs, dry fruits and sweets are also kept as a custom in some places. There is also a custom of placing a Rudra-Kalash on the *ishaana-kon* (north-east direction).

Arrival of Procession at Bride's Place (Bad-Badhaaoo)

This ritual is to inform the bride's house about the arrival of the wedding procession at their door.

The person who gives the information to the bride's house about the arrival of wedding procession at their door is called the *bad-badhaaoo*. In Rajasthan, this ritual is usually performed by a person of the barber caste only. The person who gives this message is honoured by the bride's side by tying a turban and giving sweets. He works like a messenger only.

In ancient days, this messenger's job was done by Shri Ganesh only. We still find in the old ritual songs that Ganeshji did the job of *bad-badhaaoo* during the marriage ceremonies of Shri Krishna, Shiva, Brahma, etc. In fact, this messenger was despatched before the departure of the procession. Now, though the wedding processions go in buses, the *badbadhaaoo* still occupies a prominent place.

Today, we see that large arrangements are made at the airports and railway stations to receive the wedding guests. If the procession is arriving by road, 15-20 persons from the bride's side are seen standing at least 10-15 km away to welcome them. All the members of the procession are welcomed and taken to the arrival place with full honours. As per requirement, the arrangements are made for snacks, tea and other refreshments. Also available are a barber, a cobbler and a washerman in service of the groom's guests.

Ornaments for the Bride
(Padla)

This ritual means that after the wedding procession reaches the bride's place, ornaments, clothes, bracelets, shoes and cash are sent for the bride from the groom's side.

Before the departure of the procession, at the groom's house, red carpets are spread on the floor, and the guests and close relatives are invited to take seat on them. All the items to be given to the bride, including clothes and jewellery, are spread on the floor for all to see. The guests, old and young, are requested to give their opinion about the items placed there so that if they find any shortage, or any work that has not been properly or adequately done, it could be corrected or even replaced there and then. It is these very clothes, including jewellery, which the bride has wear during the marriage. These include also the wedding dress which the bride wears during the marriage ceremony. This ritual has its own importance also because it is this wedding dress that a lady wishes to wear when leaving this world.

Big plates, numbering about five to six, are decorated before the ceremony with clothes and jewellery and taken to the bride's house amidst music and dance. At the bride's house or the place of marriage, all these large plates are kept in the centre of the courtyard. In royal families, at this programme, usually only the ladies are present. All items to be given to the bride including the clothes, jewellery, shoes, etc. are displayed. These items are repacked and sent along with the bride after the marriage ceremony is over.

There are usually 11, 21 or 51 boxes of jewellery including rings, necklaces, earrings, noserings, bangles, anklets, bracelets, etc. The bangles are from Mewar in red colour. These are also called the bangles of Chander Bai. At many places white bangles are also common. Besides the jewellery, there are boxes of cosmetics, dry fruits and cardamom, sweets, a lump of jaggery, fruit baskets, etc. for the bride.

Relatives Embracing Each Other (Milanee)

Milani means to "meet." This ritual is performed in order that relatives from both sides meet and get acquainted with each other. This bonds and strengthens the relations for the future.

During the royal weddings, when the procession reaches the bride's place, the people from the bride's side welcome their guests with flowers, garlands and perfumes. The royal family priest puts a *tilak* on their forehead and invites them into the bride's house. The groom remains atop the elephant or horse only. It is only when the bride's father and brother come and request him, and help him that he gets down. After alighting, he is made to stand on a decorated *chowkee* and honoured with a ceremonial robe and later taken to the stage where the wedding ceremonies will be performed. On one side the maid-servants of the bride sing songs and accompany the bridegroom as a ritual of honour. The other members of the groom's party are also warmly greeted and taken inside. People from the bride's side perform *milani* with the guests from the groom's side. The groom is seated on a decorated chair or throne and the bride's father or brother or a respected elder applies *tilak* on his forehead and gives gifts and cash. They embrace each other. Nowadays this ceremony, in many castes, is performed at the entrance gate only.

Welcoming the Guests (Agvaanee)

The bride's father, along with his close relatives and friends stand at the entrance and welcome the groom and his family, his close relatives and friends.

The groom is decorated with a turban, a thick gold necklace, a necklace made of pearls, a single breasted coat, a shoulder-band, waist-band, a thick bracelet, silken handkerchief, a sword, a narrow-legged pink cotton trousers, anchor cloth on his legs, light pink socks, shoes, etc. With all these adornments the groom is made to sit atop an elephant or a horse. The persons with musical instruments and bands lead the procession. The groom's father, grandfather and other senior male members remain in front of the procession. The groom's brothers, cousins and other close relatives and friends remain on either side of the horse or elephant. Following the procession are the people of the village and the attendants of the house where the marriage is taking place.

At the auspicious time, the members of the procession in their best attires get ready to acompany the *baaraat* for the bride's place. On both sides of the groom are seen his two or even four attendants. One holds an umbrella over the groom's head while another moves the fly whisk in semicircular direction. Other attendants keep a watch on the bridegroom and prevent anyone from casting an evil eye on him.

Thus, with music and dance, accompanied by the groom's guests, the *baaraat* reaches the bride's place. Nowadays, we find that the processionists indulge in music and dance on the way to the bride's place. The bride's close relatives welcome the groom and his party. On reaching the entrance gate, ritual *shloka*s and *mantra*s are recited by the family priests who are already present there. The bride's relatives welcome everyone with flowers, garlands and perfumes. Then follows light refreshment comprising snacks, tea or juices which all enjoy.

Making New Relationships (Torana and Kaaman)

The *baaraat* is received by the bride's mother with an auspicious pot kept on her head. A flickering lamp is also kept on the pot symbolic of enlightenment, enjoyment and prosperity. Before the *torana* ceremony (cracking the arched gateway) is performed, the bride's brother ties a ceremonial turban on the brother-in-law's head and gives him some cash as a token of honour.

After the welcome ceremony is over, the groom is taken near the *torana* (arched gateway), which is made of mango wood. Until the bridegroom cracks this gateway with his sword, he is not accepted as a brother-in-law or the son-in-law of that house. This *torana* ritual is also called as *torana-maaranaa* at some places. Sometimes the *torana* (the arched gateway) is also cracked by the wood taken from the *neem* tree or the jujube (*ber* or cherries) tree. This ceremony is performed by all classes of people — from royal families to the ordinary ones. Some grooms perform it riding on an elephant, while others do it riding a horse's back. This ritual depicts that a new relationship is being formed in the house, and the son-in-law has brought that message.

Among the kshatriys, this ritual also signifies valour. From the folk tales, we understand that the ritual of cracking or touching the *torana* was considered as a test for a husband's bravery. We found in writings that a *torana* was tied at the entrance to the house and at a very high place and it was announced that whosoever cracked the *torana* could marry the daughter of the household. In olden days it was an accepted custom by which anyone who occupied the main doorway of a house was considered really brave and that he was the most eligible to be the husband of the girl of the house. One folk tale about the ceremony's name mentions that the gods were forbidden from entering Puri as a demon named Torana blocked their way. The gods killed the demon, and hence the name *torana-maaranaa*. The completion of this ritual means that half the marriage ceremony is over. This *torana* (arched gate) is made by a village carpenter only. In exchange he gets a headband, a dress, cash and a gift. In the centre of the *torana* is placed a picture of Ganeshji. So, when the groom tries to crack it, he will automatically bow before the picture of Ganeshji first and then perform the *torana* ceremony. On this occasion, the relatives and friends accompanying the groom shower coins and sugar candies over his head and express happiness.

Welcome by Mother-in-law (Saasu Aarati)

This ritual (*aarati*) is performed by the bride's mother. It is made in triangle. The groom is alighted from the horse or elephant and is requested to stand on a small decorated wooden *chowkee* (stool). The bride's mother performs this ritual called the *poonkhan* ceremony. This ritual is meant to verify the physical and mental condition of the would-be son-in-law by the bride's mother. After completion of this ceremony, all materials for this ritual, including a churning-stick, a silver plough, foot-rest, a mirror, etc. are taken aside and then every ritual is performed and repeated at least four times. (The word *poonkan* is the regional translation of the Sanskrit word *pareekshaa,* meaning investigation or verification.) These are performed to study the physical, mental and intellectual state of the groom. This ritual is known as *pareekshaa* (investigation) and in some places is also called *parichhand* (the outer garments), i.e. examining the outer garments.

After the *aarati* by the bride's mother, the people from the groom's side give cash or kind as a *shagan* to the bride's mother and other close relatives present there. This is usually in cash or sometimes even in silvar coins. This ritual goes on till the bride arrives. This *aarati* goes along with the bride to her in-law's house. A mixture of wheat flour and gram flour is applied on thin strips of mango wood and bound by red-coloured threads — this is called *aarati.* At the entrance gate (*torana*), the bride's mother honours the groom with similar rituals which were earlier performed by the groom's mother before departing from their house . These rituals like worshipping the horse, feeding it with soaked gram, putting a *tilak* on the groom's forehead, applying lampblack (*kaajal*) in his eyes, etc. are all done and followed very religiously. The clever mother-in-law while applying *kaajal* sometimes pulls the nose of her would-be son-in-law as a part of the tests done on him.

Welcome by the Paternal Aunt (Bhuaa Saas)

The *bhuaa-saas* (paternal aunt of the bride) also performs this ritual and is given cash or kind as a *shagan* by the groom's family. The *shagan* amount varies as per family status.

Welcome by the Attendants (Daavde Samelaa)

The attendants at the bride's place get together and receive the groom with a silver pot decorated with mango leaves. They get gifts from the groom's side for performing this ritual.

Welcome by the Barber (Naayee Samelaa)

The family barber performs this ritual and welcomes the groom by bringing for him a brass pot decorated with mango leaves, etc. He too gets a suitable gift from the groom's side.

Welcome by the Band Masters (Dhol Samelaa)

This welcome ritual is performed at the entrance gate by the band masters with small clay pots decorated with mango leaves, etc. They too are given suitable gifts by the groom's side.

On this *torana* ritual, the singing of the *kaaman* songs (of Rajasthan) is a must and cannot be avoided. It is said that these ritual songs have certain spiritual powers which make the bridegroom always attached to his in-law's house. In fact, these ritual songs work like unseen sacred magical verses that help in creating an everlasting marriage bond of love and respect between the bride and the groom, especially in Rajasthan. These songs were supposedly sung by lustful women (or *kaaminee),* hence the name *kaaman.*

Testing the Groom (Vara ko Poonkhnaa)

This ritual is meant to test the groom's eligibility, eloquence and patience, besides his mental, physical and intellectual abilities. In this ritual even the groom's sisters-in-law and the bride's friends take part. They all, in a lighter mood, crack jokes, laugh, enjoy and jocularly even tease the groom. In the meantime, the bride is getting ready for going to the marriage *mandap* adorning herself with new clothes and gold ornaments. The senior ladies present, like the bride's aunts, both maternal and paternal, jocularly measure the groom's shoulder and share some light moments with him. This is also said to be a kind of ritual of ancient days which tests the wittiness and patience of the groom. On the day of the marriage, at the auspicious time the bride is given the ceremonial bath and made to wear new wedding clothes and ornaments from head to feet. All the elders bless the girl. The girl's mother puts a *tilak* on the girl's forehead as a mark of consecration of marriage and makes her seek the blessings of the family god-goddess, for a very long life as a married woman with all prosperity.

Worshipping and Tying of Sacred Knot (Maayaam mein Poojan and Gathajoraa)

सिद्धिदाता सुतो यस्या स्वयं सौभाग्यदायिनी ।
वर-कन्या-परग्रंथि बन्धने सुखदा भवेत ॥

siddhidaataa suto yasyaa
svayam saubhaagyadaayinee ।
vara-kanyaa-paragranthi
bandhane sukhadaa bhavet ॥

This ritual means to finally unite the bride and the groom in a sacred relationship for eternity. The groom is brought to place of the ceremony (*maayaam*) where the bride has already been seated. They both are made to sit on two decorated silver stools next to each other — the bride sits on the left side of the groom. The royal family priest begins the henna ritual. Under this ritual, the priest wishes that the new couple should lead a long, happy, loving, peaceful and prosperous life. A *svastika* is made on a stone slab. A few leaves of henna and wood-apple leaves, are rubbed along with vermilion on this slab to make a colour. Then the priest takes out some bangles worn by the gods-goddesses and and put them in the bride's wrist. Then he ties on the wrists of both the bride and the groom a sacred thread of red colour (*mauli* or *kaankan dolaraa*), and utters this *shloka* —

मंगलम् भगवान् विष्णुर्मंगलं गरूड़ध्वजः ।
मंगलम् पुण्डरीकाक्षो सर्वमंगलायस्तनो हरिः ॥

मंगलम् भगवान् विष्णुर्मंगलं गरूड़ध्वजः ।
हरिर्मांगल्यकृद् भूयाद् वरवध्वो करगृहे: ॥

mangalam bhagavaan vishnur
mangalam garudadhvajah ।
mangalam pundareekaaksho
sarvamangalaayastano harih ॥
mangalam bhagavaan vishnur
mangalam garudadhvajah ।
harirmaangalyakrid bhooyaad
varavadhvo karagraheh ॥

The right hand side lower edge of the bride's veil is tied with the left hand lower edge of the groom's *dupattaa* in a sacred knot, with the remaining portion of the *dupattaa* passing over the groom's right shoulder from the back. For this ritual, a light pink or a red coloured cotton cloth is used to tie and cover the knot. The sacred knot signifies that both the couple remain together united like this knot forever. It is also called *granthi bandhan.*

The actual meaning of this ritual is that the couple's mind and body should work together in harmony. Now at this present moment both of them are one, and united together and it is wished that they remain like that for all time to come. That is the reason why this sacred knot is considered very important in any marriage ceremony. This knot is also considered to be never breaking.

Five items are contained inside this knot. They are: coins (paise), flowers (*pushpa*), turmeric (*haldee*), soft green grass (*doorvaa*) and rice grains (*chaaval*). According to marriage rituals, these five items are very important and have special significance as explained below:

1. **Coins (*paise*)** — It signifies that there would be no independent control over money and that there would always be joint control only. Whatever will be spent shall be done with mutual consent only.
2. **Flowers (*pushpa*)** — This signifies happiness and prosperity — to lead such a beautiful life always, to feel happy on seeing each other, always praise the other partner and never criticize your partner.
3. **Turmeric (*haldee*)** — This signifies health and veneration. To have concern and care for each other's healthy life. Always be happy and respectful to each other. Keep the mind away from narrow feelings.
4. **Green grass (*doorvaa*)** — This signifies that love between the two should never fade, whatever situation may arise. It is significant to note that the grass always remains green and fresh. Even when it dries up, by putting it in a little water, it again freshens. Similarly, the new couple should always remain soft, lively, green and fresh as the grass. They should have an unending bond like the moon (*chandra*) and the partridge (*chakora*) bird who are always ready to sacrifice for each other.
5. **Rice grains (*akshata* or *chaaval*)** — This signifies food. Whatever food is consumed through earnings, should be consumed mutually only. Responsibility towards family, society and the country should always be kept in mind. It is also wished that the bride will always support the groom and remain with him in all his joys and sorrows. That is why the grains of rice are tied in the sacred knot.

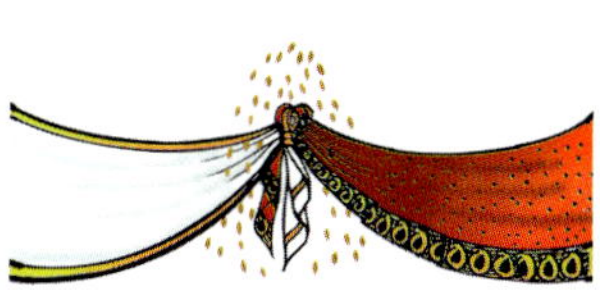

The Hand-taking Ceremony (Hathalevaa)

This ritual signifies the mutual hand-taking ceremony between the bride and the groom.

This hand-taking (*hathalevaa* or *hasta-milaap*) is a very significant ritual in any marriage ceremony. At the most auspicious time, this ritual is performed. The couple — the bride and the groom — with an emotional feeling extend their hands toward each other and take a vow before the whole society to live together. The groom extends both his hands and grips the bride's hand tightly. It seems that he has been physically and emotionally attached to her. He vows to live with her on all occasions and in all happenings, and will remain steadfast in the interest of his bride only. As such he "surrenders" his hands in the hands of his bride-to-be for ever.

Ritually, in the right hands of both the bride and the groom, a little henna paste and a coin are placed and the hands are tied with a saffron coloured cloth. The *mauli* (red sacred thread) is tied on both their wrists by the family's royal priest. The henna for this ceremony that is used is the one gifted by the bride's side along with other items. All this is done amidst the recitation of verses and chanting of mantras by the priest. Sisters of the bride help in making this henna paste. The sister is given a *saari* and the brother-in-law is given a suit along with cash. After the hand-taking ceremony the couple again proceeds to the *lagna mandap.* Some people prefer that this ritual be performed by their family *guru* instead of the priest. For this ceremony the bride is decked in a *saree* given by her maternal uncle, which is called korajalya.

Once the hand-taking ceremony has been done the hands of both are separated only after the complete marriage ceremony is over.

Circumambulation of Fire — Agni Pradakshinaa (Phere)

This ritual means that both the bride and the groom circumambulate the fire and pray to the Fire God (Agnideva).

At the auspicious *mandap* (pavilion), the bride and the groom are asked to take their seats. Their parents, grandparents and other close relatives sit opposite to them on cushioned seats for the *kanyaadaan*. The royal family priest sits in the northern direction of the bride. The bride and the groom circumambulate the place three times amidst the chant of *mantra*s by the priest. Up to three rounds, the bride leads, but from the fourth round she follows the groom. The brother or the maternal uncle of the bride performs the *sevare* ritual (rotating a lamp in a circular form) before the groom. It is a kind of honouring the groom. Later the bride's brother performs the *kataaree* ritual, i.e. taking out the groom's sword from the sheath. The bride's brother returns the sword to his brother-in-law with full honours but only after receiving a gift or cash from him.

From the fourth up to the seventh circumambulation, the ceremony becomes very emotional, especially for the bride's side. At this time, all the ladies on the bride's side and other ladies present sing ritual songs of *aambaa paakaa* and *an aamalee* meaning that from today the daughter is separated and has become the member of another family.

Circumambulating around the sacrificial fire is the real essence of the marriage ritual. Taking seven rounds of this fire is religiously most important and is the very base of these rituals which are continuing for the last several thousand years. Under this ceremony, both the bride and the groom circumambulate the fire, and take a vow before the Agnideva (the fire god), all relatives, and close friends that they mutually accept this religious bonding and shall do their best to maintain it by living together with love and respect towards each other, and that they shall leave no stone unturned in maintaining it with utmost care. This ritual is performed in the presence of fire and before the fire God (Agnideva) because it is this very fire that is not only the essence of our life but also has a great potential which gives us speed, progress, health, etc. on this planet and makes our life comfortable and enjoyable.

When the bride and the groom are taken to this place of circumambulation (*mandap*), they are seated facing the eastern direction. The bride is asked to sit on the southern or right-hand side of the groom. The parents of the bride are sitting facing either the north or the west direction. Here too, the bride's mother sits on the southern or right hand side of her husband, and a sacred knot is also tied between them (bride's parents).

Spiritually, it is said that *agni* (fire) on earth is the representative of sun. The sun is the soul of this world and a representative of Lord Vishnu. Therefore, to circumambulate the *agni* (fire) means circumbulating the Almighty God itself. Fire destroys all our evils. To begin an important work in life, it is very important and beneficial to start the work in the presence of fire (*agni*) only. During the recitation of *shloka*s (verses), the groom addresses the bride thus:

> हे वधू। मैं सामवेद के समान हूँ। तू ऋग्वेद के समान है। तू पृथ्वी की तरह क्षमाशील और लोक व्यवहार करने वाली है। मैं सूर्य के समान निरन्तर श्रम करने वाला हूँ।
>
> O bride ! I am like *Saamaveda* and you are like *Rigveda*. You, like the earth, will remain cool and forgiving always, and remain in social life, whereas I like the sun, will work hard continously and regularly.

The circumambulation comprises seven rounds. Initially the bride leads the three rounds. After this, the groom leads. But one of the rounds, the fourth, is performed together and in such a way that both the bride and the groom circumambulate, i.e. take half round each, thus completing the full circle. After the completion of every round, the family priest recites the verses concerning that part of the ceremony. Marriage is a religious ritual to be performed properly and with care and interest. During this ceremony, besides the recitation of Vedic verses, the sacrificial fire (*yagya*) is lit and made the witness to the whole ceremony.

The marriage ceremony is such a pure, pious and sacred ritual that to successfully perform this ritual, learned priests are called who have thorough knowledge of Vedas and verses. Besides reciting them, they should also be able to explain their meaning to all present during the whole ceremony. The recitation of verses should be so melodious and heart-touching that it catches the concentration of all present, and the bride and the groom in particular. In-between, the bride's father worships the groom in the form of Lord Vishnu. According to our scriptures, during the performance of marriage ritual *poorna aahuti*, i.e. the ritual of performing complete oblation, is not done for the reason that it is the beginning of a new life for the bride and the groom.

Initially, for first three rounds, the bride is shown in a leading role because it is only the woman who conrols the family and the household affairs by her experience. The works like service, trading and those done outside the house, are usually performed by the man only, and therefore, for three rounds the woman follows the man. Both within the house and outside, both man and woman should lead lives in complete harmony between them. Later, the priest addresses the bride thus:

> हे वत्से! यही अग्नि देव तुम्हारे विवाह के साक्षी हैं। तुम्हें अपने पति के साथ गृहस्थाश्रम के धार्मिक कृत्यों को पूर्ण करना है।

O daughter! This God Agni is witness to your marriage. You, along with your husband, have to lead a cordial domestic life fulfilling all the family responsibilities together.

Earlier to this, a tale of Shiva-Paarvati is narrated by the priest to both of them. How Sati longed and craved to marry Shiva, and only desired that somehow, by hook or crook, Shiva should become her husband. But when Sati's father King Daksha, rebuked and insulted his son-in-law (Shiva), she says, while jumping into the *agni-kunda* (sacrificial fire pit) at her very own father's house, that in all her births she wants only Shiva as her husband.

Hiding the Shoes (Joote Chhipaanaa)

This is yet another lighter moment of sport in marriages. Amidst fun and frolic, the groom's shoes are taken away by the bride's side and hidden.

Nowadays, this sport has become very common which in fact makes the otherwise sad and sombre atmosphere cheerful to some extent. The bride's younger sisters, cousins, friends, nieces and nephews all are party to this mischief.

When the groom sits for the circumambulation (*phere*) ceremony, he opens his shoes before taking his place. The bride's younger sisters take away one shoe of the groom and hide it somewhere. This leads to a lot of fun, frolic, laughter and enjoyment. The groom and his side plead before these girls to return them his shoe. It is only after receiving several requests and taking a suitable price for it, that the shoe is returned to the groom.

Climbing the Mountain (Parvataarohana)

The groom urges his bride to be as firm as a rock in righteousness or *dharmaa yathaa ashvamevam sthir bhava*. As a ritual, till the completion of the third circumambulation (*phere*) ceremony, the bride firmly puts her foot on a rock placed on the circumambulation path. This rock is compared to a horse which signifies steadiness, strength and victory; while the rock signifies solidity and firmness. The groom tells the bride to keep her foot on the rock and even compares her to a goddess. He tells her to be strong and sturdy as this rock in her household *dharma*. She should suppress the corrupt, the trouble-makers and the jealous.

In this way, the groom forewarns his bride that such circumstances may come in life and that she will have to win over all of them firmly. Before the beginning of the fourth round (*phere*), the rock is removed, as that was kept ritually only for the bride for the first three rounds. From fourth round onwards, she follows the groom till the end of the ceremony.

Hand-taking and the Vows (Paanigrahan and Vachana)

The bride's father invites the groom to take the hand of the bride and exchange vows that both will live their married life together for ever.

After the circumambulation (*phere*) ceremony is over, till the bride comes to the left side of the groom ritually, she is deemed to be unmarried. As per our ancient scriptures, a man is born out of the right shoulder of Brahma (the Creator) and a woman from his left shoulder. Therefore, a woman is also called by the name *vaamaangee* (person on the left) and after the marriage, the woman is given her place on the left side of her husband. Up to the seventh circumambulation (*phere*), the bride is made to sit on the right side of the groom because till that time she is considered an outsider. When she takes the matrimonial vows and is bound with the groom, she becomes a wife and is made to sit on the left side of her husband. Now, she becomes an important actor or personality in the husband's family. This act is also called the "change of posture" (*aasan parivartan*), i.e. the bride and the groom exchange their seats.

According to Lord Manu, before the creation took place, the Almighty divided himself into two parts. Which part became the male and which turned into the female, is mentioned in detail in

Devi Bhaagavata —

स्वेच्छामय: स्वेच्छयायं द्विधारूपो बभूव ह: ।
स्त्री रूपो वामभागांशो दक्षिणांश: पुमान् स्मृत: ॥

svecchaamayah svecchayaayam
dvidhaaroopo babhoova hah ।
stree roopo vaamabhaagaamsho
dakshinaamshah pumaan smritah ॥

meaning, the self-willing Amighty took two forms — the left side created the female, while the right side the male.

Here the verse of Lord Ganesha is recited.

विघ्नेश्वराय वरदाय सुरप्रियाय,
लम्बोदराय सकलाय लगद्धिताय ।
नागाननाय सितसर्पविभूषिताय,
गौरीसुताय गणनाथ नमो नमस्ते ॥
अनया पूजया ऋद्धिसिद्धि-सहित:
श्री गणपति: प्रियताम् ।

vighneshvaraaya varadaaya surapriyaaya,
lambodaraaya sakalaaya lagaddhitaaya ।
naagaananaaya sitasarpavibhooshitaaya,
gaureesutaaya gananaatha namo namaste ॥
anayaa poojayaa riddhi-siddhi-sahitah
Shri ganapatih preeyataam ।

The couples are made in heaven. On earth, only the rituals are being followed. Since the union of soul is pre-determined, on earth only the various rituals are being performed giving it another form. The bride's father, taking some water, which contains the five elements, in his hand, addresses the groom saying, "this is my daughter, your co-traveller, accept her hand. She is very chaste and highly reputed. She will always follow you like a shadow."

Saying this he pours the water. Here six verses are recited and both the bride and the groom are bound by the vows completely. After taking these vows, both take a pledge to live together, work together and keep up the sacred relationship throughout their life. The bride also seeks seven vows from the groom thus —

1. In pilgrimage, fasting, festivities, *yagya*, charity, etc. promise that you will remain with me and support me so that I may come to your left and be your wife;
2. If you worship your ancestors by performing sacrifices and giving food and charity to Brahmans, and worship your parents, promise me that in the same way you will honour my parents, so that I may come to your left and be your wife;
3. You promise to protect the family and its cattle, so that I may come to your left and be your wife;
4. You assure me that you will manage the household with your earnings and keep the store full of grains, so that I may come to your left and be your wife;
5. You promise to do charitable work by building temples, gardens, tanks, wells, etc. so that I may come to your left and be your wife;
6. If you perform any trade and commercial activity in this city or in any other city, you will do so after asking me, only then I may come to your left and be your wife; and finally
7. You promise that will not touch or see any other woman with passion or wrong intentions, so that I may come to your left and be your wife.

In this way, the bride takes seven vows from the groom. In return, the groom takes only one vow from his bride —

As long as I am at home, you will indulge in sports and pass time playfully and joyfully adorning your body with turmeric paste, cream, perfume, etc. and you will take part in social functions, go to temples, and visit neighbours and even unknown places. But when I am not at home and away in a foreign place, you will just forget all these activities and turn your face away from all these. Vishnu, Agni, the pole star, family priests, my courteous brothers, and various other members of the family are all with me and support me. You act according to my wishes, and do not go against my words. Whatever I say, keep it in your mind. This way uphold the *pativrat dharma* (right ways of a chaste wife). Along with these, be modest and courteous, and speak softly and sweetly, serve your father-in-law and mother-in-law, follow the right path and keep trust in God. Do the things which make me happy. Treat my brothers and other relatives with respect and honour. Obey my instructions and become worthy of my trust in you. Then you will be called my *vaamaangee* (left half of my body), i.e. a part of me. If you follow my mind and act according to my wishes, I promise that I will do whatever you say. A home without a wife is incomplete. Therefore, today I keep all my faith in you and accept you on my left side.

After this, the bride is taken through the front side of the groom and seated on his left. This implies that from now onwards, the wife will never cross her husband from the front and will only follow him.

The family priest opens the cloth binding the right hands of the bride and groom and places the bride's hand into the groom's. The priest requests all the relatives of the bride present to perform the ritual of *kanyaadaan* (giving daughter's hand in marriage). First, the parents of the bride are called to perform this ritual by giving a cow in charity (*gaudaana*) and initiate the ceremony. After this, all the relatives present give their blessings and *shagan* (cash) to both the bride and the groom. The bride's unmarried sisters or cousin-sisters perform *aarati* (worship) to both of them. Guests from the groom's side keep *shagan* (cash) on the *aarati* plate (a plate containing a lit lamp, some sweets and flowers, etc). This *shagan* goes to the girls who perform the *aarati*.

Filling Vermilion and Wearing Wedding Thread (Maangbharaayee and Mangalsutra)

The groom with a silver coin fills the bride's hair parting on the head with vermilion (*kumkum*). He also ties a wedding thread (*mangalsutra*) around her neck. A married lady or a priest brings a small box containing vermilion and a silver coin. The groom picks up the coin and dips it in the vermilion and applies it (or fills) on the hair-parting on the bride's head. This ritual is also called the *sumangali* (good and auspicious) ritual. After this, the married woman regularly puts vermilion on her hair-parting throughout her life wishing a long and blessed life for her husband. In Hinduism this ritual is being followed very religiously, signifying that the lady with vermilion on her hair-parting is a married woman with her husband living.

Vermilion on a woman's hair-parting not only brightens her personality but also signifies auspiciousness. It also conveys and signifies that Brahma is ever glowing and the glow's colour is red. In *Devi Bhaagavata,* there is a mention by the Goddess Bhagvati herself that Brahma and herself (Shakti) are one and the same, and combined together they created this world. Devi or Shakti has a liking for the red colour.

Our scriptures mention this vermilion ceremony as very sacred as its place is just above the

Brahmarandhra (opening at the top of the skull through which the soul, after death, is said to escape and gets united with the Absolute). This vulnerable place is also called the place of Eternal Truth and is more delicate in women as compared to men. Due to the presence of high content of mercury in the vermilion, the face always glows and wrinkles do not appear early. It also helps the women keep active and energetic throughout the day, and protects this vulnerable spot from bad influences from outside. The mercury content also helps in destroying the louse and dandruff from the person's head.

Along with the performance of the vermilion ceremony, the groom puts a *mangalsutra* (wedding thread) around his bride's neck. She wears this thread as long as her husband is alive. It is believed that this *mangalsutra* (wedding thread) and vermilion (*kumkum*) on hair-parting can never be separated from a woman as long as her husband is alive. It is priceless and can never be replaced by any other jewellery. It is only after the death of her husband, that the woman takes it out.

The making of this thread requires black colour beads strewn in a string. Addition of gold coins (*mohar*) and a locket is also a must. It is believed that the coin reflects the pure love and care for her husband and the locket gives protection to her husband from any inauspicious happening. The black beads protect the woman from evil eyes and also prevent the energy released from her body from being destroyed.

There is also a religious importance behind wearing this wedding thread (*mangalsutra*) by women. It is believed that once it is worn it is never taken out. The women consider it very inauspicious if the thread is broken or if it is lost.

Daughter's Marriage Rite (Kanyaadaan)

The parents and elder relatives of an unmarried girl give their daughter's hand to a groom in marriage.

After the completion of the circumambulation ceremony (*phere*) around the fire and the ritual of releasing the hands, the relatives present give cash and kind as gift to the couple. After this the father of the bride performs the ritual of *kanyaadaan* by addressing the groom and saying that he is like Lord Vishnu and that he should accept the hand of his daughter and bring her good fortune. In fact, *kanyaadaan* is a ritual on which the foundation of a family is based and which brings progress and prosperity. It is said *kanyaadaan* is *mahaadaana*, meaning giving the daughter in marriage is the biggest and the noblest act of charity that one can perform on this planet. It is also said that all of us donate gold, silver and other valuable things, but giving a daughter in marriage is above all of them. On the marriage day, the parents of the bride or the couple who performs the *kanyaadaan* ritual keep fast till the end of the ceremony. But it is not advisable for the bride and the groom to remain on fast on this day. The society in India considers it an honour and a privilege to perform this *kanyaadaan* ritual. Both the literate and illiterate people perform this ritual with full fervour and gaiety. They give the most precious possessions of their life to the daughter and perform this ritual. The money and other possessions are also called *kanyaadhan* (the daughter's wealth).

Kanyaadaan is the most important and virtuous ceremony ever performed by any person in his life. It is said that the merit attained by digging ten wells is equal to constructing one tank. Constructing ten such tanks is equal to the merit of digging one reservior. Building ten such reserviors is equal to one *kanyaadaan* (giving a daughter in marriage), because for the person who is donating a daughter, his life and virtues grow manifold. For the person who receives the gift (of a girl), i.e. the groom, his strength, vigour for the living years increase. As a token of acceptance of the gift (*kanyaa*) the bridegroom gives solemn promises and some cash (*dakshinaa*).

Kanyaadaan is the life's greatest dream of all parents. The daughter whom they nurtured and brought up with so much care and love is one day given away in marriage to an unknown person. The moment is very emotional — heart of the parents sinks, their hands tremble and they repeatedly pray to the Almighty to give peace and prosperity to their daughter. They are equally satisfied that their daughter will begin a new life and in a new family, and that too in an altogether new atmosphere like they did when they were married, and that her clan will now be identified not by her father's, but by her husband's. She will attain a new name, new family, a new look altogether.

Walking Seven Steps Together (Saptapadee)

After the completion of the ritual of the seven circumambulations around the sacred fire, the bride and the groom perform the ceremony of walking together the first time the seven steps and begin their new life.

Before this ceremony, preparations are made by making seven small heaps of rice grains. The couple move one step at a time, stop and move their second step ahead. In this way they together complete the seven steps, the first of their lives together. On the completion of every step, the family priest chants some *mantra*s. Both the bride and the groom, in the presence of various gods and relatives, perform this ritual which ultimately benefits them throughout their life. With every step the couple take, the feelings expressed are as follows:

First step is taken for the growth of food. Diet has a special significance and relation with good health. Therefore, nutritious food is very important.

Second step is taken for physical and mental growth.

Third step is taken for growth of wealth. For improving the economic status, wealth is very important. This can be gained with hard work both by the wife and the husband.

Fourth step is taken for seeking the growth of happiness. The couple wish for lifelong satisfaction and a pleasant life.

Fifth step is taken for the proper performance of all duties. This includes looking after the welfare of all family members, those who take refuge in the household, and all birds and animals.

Sixth step is taken for proper regimen according to seasons, i.e. following the right method, manner and custom of living.

Seventh step is taken for the wife's obedience to her husband, politeness and friendly nature. Here, the husband also promises and agrees to be noble, kind, friendly towards his wife and to be her follower always in life. In case anything goes wrong between the two, the help of polite and kind words like "sorry," "excuse me," etc. are to be made use of so that their marital life remains smooth, stress-free, steady and progresses without any hindrance.

Family Genealogies (Shaakhochchaar)

This is a ritual of giving blessings by all the elders present to both the new husband and wife after they have been bound in a sacred knot.

After completion of the ceremonies, *maangbharaayi* (putting vermilion by groom on the bride's hair-parting and tying of *mangalasutra* (the sacred black thread) to the bride by the groom, the priest mentions about the exogamous sub-division of a caste-group (*gotra*) that both the bride and the groom belong to. Then the ladies present crack a joke on the priest's scholarly erudition and say jocularly —

भलो पढ्यो रे पांड्या भलो पढ्यो । जजमाना री गीत पढ्यो ॥

bhalo padhyo re paandyaa bhalo padhyo ।
jajamaanaa ree geet padhyo ॥

meaning, "the priest is a real knowledgeable person, a real learned scholar. The Brahman even sang the song."

On this occasion, ritual songs are also sung signifying that an auspicious ceremony has ended successfully.

At this moment, the mother of the bride performs the *aarati* (worship) of the new couple. In turn the bride also worships both her parents. At last the couple fold their hands and respecfully greet and thank everyone present there. All of them shower blessings on the couple and wish for their healthy, wealthy, peaceful, prosperous and progressive life. They also place some rice grains on the couple's heads. After the culmination of the ceremony, the fathers of both bride and the groom give cash and kind in charity.

Prayers by the Bride (Laavaavidhaan)

By this ritual, the bride prays for the long life of her husband, for the welfare, progress and prosperity of the whole family, and wishes to live with mutual love and respect.

From the groom's side, two or three brothers of the groom are called to the ritual place (*lagna mandap*). The barber from the side of the groom enters holding a tray in his hand containing dry fruits and coins. As the couple finally gets up after completing the rituals, dry fruits and coins are tossed in the air over their heads by the barber. The attendants and other helpers of the bride's house rush to collect them. This ritual of tossing dry fruits and coins in the air over the couple's head is called *mendaa barsaanaa*.

At some places, the ritual of *laavaavidhaan* is also performed. The newly married couple stand facing the sacred fire. In between them from behind, the bride's brother takes some puffed rice along with *palaash* leaves dipped in ghee and fills his sister's joined arms with them. The bride standing in front puts these items into the sacred fire. The priest chants some *mantras*. This is done three times. With these *mantras* the bride prays:

> Almighty, I am sacrificing my parent's house and entering my husband's home. Let me not be

separated from my husband. May my husband have a very long life. May my father's and my husband's homes remain always filled with all kinds of significant wealth. May my love for my husband remain unbroken, I pray to God for the same.

We have already read above that out of the seven circumambulations (*phere*) around the sacred fire, the initial three *phere*s are led by the bride, and that the bride stands in the front while doing the *laajaa hom*. The significance behind is that when the union of the two souls is taking place, Kaamadeva, the God of Love, releases his unerring arrows to dislodge them in copulation. In order to defuse his efforts and to ensure that nothing inauspicious happens, the woman is kept in the front. It is well known that a brave man never attacks an unarmed woman. Moreover, a man's love takes the form of a wife and completes all jobs.

The groom goes round the fire holding his bride's hand which signifies that he takes a vow to complete every work with the co-operation and participation of his partner only. And that she will always be consulted and kept along with him in fulfilling any work. Also it is vowed before the God Agni that from now on all their five sense organs will work hand-in-hand. Whatever items are left after the third oblation, the bride puts them into the fire as the fourth oblation (*aahuti*) to Kamadeva (God of Love). These initial four oblations are performed by the bride only, who wishes a healthy and long life for her husband. The bride's brothers also wish for their dear sister's happy married life and thus take part in all the ritual ceremonies.

Observing the Pole Star or the Sun (Dhruva Taaraa or Surya Darshana)

The bridegroom shows to his bride the pole star, which remains fixed on the sky and says that their relationship should be permanent like the pole star and bright like the sun.

If the marriages are performed during the night, the groom requests the bride to have a look at the pole star. And if the marriage ceremony is solemnized during day, he asks his bride to look at the sun. After seeing the sun or the pole star, they both take a vow that like the pole star or the sun their relationship will remain firm, steady, strong and shining forever. As we know both the pole star and the sun are permanently fixed in their places in the sky.

After taking a vow, both the bride and the groom take a pledge to live together happily for hundred years. Later they both are bathed with the waters from Rudra Kalash or the sacred pitcher kept in the marriage *mandap*. The groom places his hands on the shoulders of his bride and says "May my and your hearts become one, may my and your minds become one." They also together pray : "O, God, may Vaayu or air join both our *praan*s (breath) and let us work in unison, one for the other; may Brahma and Kaamadeva unite us together and make us into one."

Bowing Down at the Sacred Place (At Maayaam or Kohabar)

After the marriage rituals are over, both the bride and the groom bow their heads at the sacred place. The bride and the groom are accompanied from the makeshift marriage stage (*vedikaa*) and brought to the sacred place (*maayaam*) where other rituals were performed and which is the place of Lord Ganeshji. They enter this place and together bow down their heads and request Lord Ganeshji to bless them with a successful, peaceful and prosperous life together. The priest congratulates them and gives his blessings to the couple.

The women present there share jokes and ask the groom some light questions and thus start some entertainment with him. The groom tries to evade some of the questions, while to some he answers smartly. Sometimes when the groom does not speak, the women ask him if he was dumb. Even they comment on him if he is hard of hearing and speak loudly or sometimes very softly, thus making the whole atmosphere full of fun and frolic. In this way the women test the patience of the groom and make a lighter mood all around.

Fasting on the Marriage Day (Kanyaavrat)

On the marriage day, the elderly male and female members on the bride's side keep fast. They break their fast and consume food only after all the marriage ceremonies are over successfully. This fast that is kept on this day, is called *kanyaavrat* or *kanyaaval*. The vow of fast is taken at the time the pillar or *dhaanee* is erected.

On this day, some people from the bride's side even consume sweet food made from the flour of water chest-nut (*singhaaraa*) and the butter liquid prepared with rock-salt. This is the only fast on the side of the bride which is kept with complete faith and devotion. It is prayed and wished that the ceremony should finish peacefully and satisfactorily. After the ceremony is over, all the relatives of the bride who have kept fast, together consume food. The water from the pitcher that was offered earlier at the time of *thaam*, pillar-laying ceremony, is also consumed while preparing this food.

Prohibiting Groom's Entry (Javaaeen Dvaar-Rokaayee)

After the completion of all marriage ceremonies, the groom takes his bride to the temporary residence of baraat (*janvaasaa*). The sons-in-law (*javaaeen*) of the house stop them from entering just for fun.

This ceremony is performed when the groom accompanies his bride and takes her to *janvaasaa* for the first time. This *janvaasaa* is the very place from where the wedding procession earlier started for the bride's place. The sons-in-law together stop the couple from entering the house. They deliberately delay their entry. It is only after the groom or his father gives cash or gift to the sons-in-law do they allow them to enter the house. Lot of bargaining to reduce the amount to be gifted from both sides takes place on this occasion. Also one can see many requests and pleas being made to the sons-in-law to allow the couple to enter. But ultimately the groom accepts defeat and has to pay the price demanded by his brothers-in-law.

Ritual of Bearing Children (Gaud Bharnaa)

This is a ritual for bearing children and is performed by the father-in-law upon his daughter-in-law.

After the marriage ceremony is over, the bride is taken by the groom to the *janvaasaa* place. She is gaud taken to a safe place in the *janvaasaa* where the groom's father or elder brother performs this ceremony of *god bharnaa* (a ritual blessing for bearing children). They keep dry fruits and cash in the bride's lap and give their blessings. The bride bows before them and seeks their blessings in return. She then mingles with the guests and relatives present.

She stays in the *janvaasaa* for some time only. After a few hours, she is again brought back to her parents' house. The significance behind this ritual is that the newly married bride is blessed to be happy at all times and that her lap should always be full, indirectly meaning that she should have many children.

Untying the Ritual Threads (Kaankan Dolade Kholanaa)

On this occasion, *doladaa* (threads, shells, beads, etc.) that were earlier tied to the groom's hands are opened by the bride. As she faces difficulty in untying the thread containing so many small knots she is made to realize the obstacles that may come in life and the efforts she should make to overcome them with patience.

Before the beginning of the marriage rituals, in both the bride and the groom's hands and feet some ritual threads are tied. These are tied on the right hand and foot of the groom and on the left hand and foot of the bride. The bride says to the groom,

O Lord! I am tied in various bonds since time immemorial. Today, I have come to seek your shelter. Kindly accept me by releasing all my bindings. May your character glow so much with virtues and nobility that I may soon be freed from all bondages.

On this occasion, the ritual threads of the groom are opened by the bride and those of the bride by her groom. The bride can use both her hands while the groom has to use only one hand for untying these threads. The one who unties all the threads earlier is declared the winner. This ritual also signifies that in their real lives both of them will together overcome the difficulties and succeed ultimately. These ritual threads are tied seven times on the hands and feet of both the bride and the groom. Even this is a fun ritual that is played with joy and enthusiasm.

After completing all these rituals, comes the lunch time. From the bride's side, her sisters and her younger sisters-in-law (*bhaabhis*) take part. Several silver plates are kept on the decorated silver stools. Food of five varieties is kept in these plates. Both the bride and the groom remove some food from their plates and feed each other. Likewise, the other guests who are present also give some food to the bride and the groom. This ceremony is called the *kava* ceremony. During lunch time the mood is joyful. Outside the dining room/hall the attendants and other lady helpers are busy singing ritual songs. After partaking food, the groom's side gives cash and gifts which all the cooks and the attendants share.

Playing a Game of Gambling (Juaa-jui-kaudhee Khel)

Only for the sake of enjoyment this game is played ritually. After the consumption of food, it is again time to have fun and frolic with both the bride and the groom. They both are made to sit at the ritual place again, this time to play a game of *juaa-jui* (a game of gambling). The groom's patience and his attitude towards his elders and youngsters are also tested through this ritual. In a large circular metal dish having raised edges, some buttermilk mixed with water is poured. Also are mixed in this solution some dry fruits, sea-shells and a ring. The bride and the groom have to take out the ring from this vessel. This routine is repeated seven times and each time both of them have to take out the ring. The person who wins more times, gets the ring. Usually this sport goes in favour of the bride only.

Besides the above sport, the attendants in the presence of all relatives bring a similar dish, but containing water mixed with turmeric powder. In this yellow-coloured water they mix many small shells, coins and also a ring. Then the chief attendant asks both the bride and the groom to take out the ring from the solution. Several times the ring is in the hand of the attendant only and she enjoys the play. This is also played seven times. The person who wins more times is declared the winner. In this game, usually the groom is made to win.

The message given by this sport is that if one is alert and active, he can be successful in life too. The ritual is followed only to convey this message to the newly married couple and to wish both of them good luck and a successful life.

Picking up the Cotton Swabs (Ruee ke Phohe Choonnaa)

This ritual is also for fun. Bodies of the groom and the bride are stuck with cotton swabs and they both are asked to pick them up from each other's body.

In ancient days, picking up cotton swabs from the fields was considered a very important activity. After the crop had ripened, all the ladies of the house gathered in a group and would go to the fields to pick-up the cotton swabs. They would bring home the collected cotton swabs in a big bundle, clean them, spin them into yarns and send them to the mills for making cloth. This ritual of safely picking up the cotton swabs and bringing them home was known as *kabjaa.* Thus began the cotton swab picking up ritual.

In this ceremony, the *naayan* (a barber's wife) would stick big size cotton swabs all over the bodies of the groom first and then the bride. At the prescribed time, the bride and the groom have to remove these swabs from each other's body. This ritual sport is played five times each, first on the body of the groom and then five time on the body of the bride. Under this sport, each swab has to be removed from the other's body carefully. The person who removes the swabs in lesser time is the winner. The part(s) of the cotton left on the body is not counted. Sometimes bride and groom, pretending to pick up swabs, pinch each other in a frolicking mood. This sport, in fact, is played only to bring closeness between the couple by giving them an opportunity to touch each other's body.

Circumambulating the Bed and Changing Seats (Palangaachaar and Paataa-Pher)

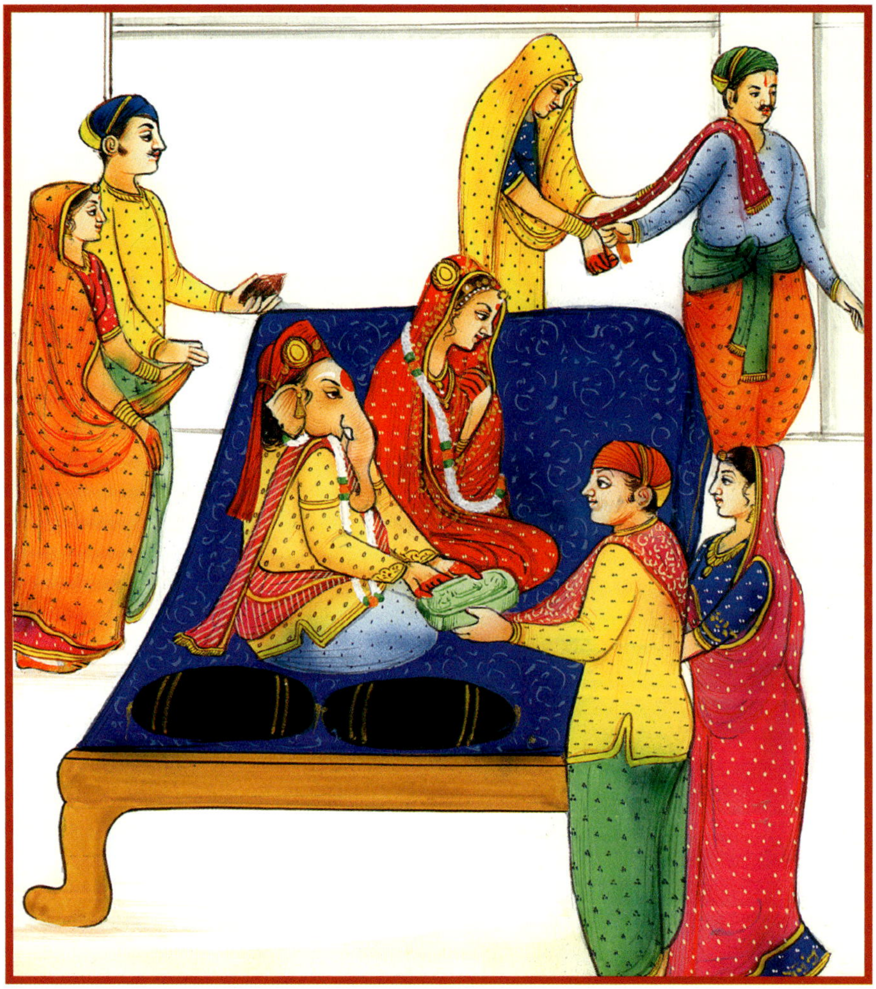

The bride and the groom are considered as Lord Vishnu and Goddess Lakshmi and circumambulated by all the members present in the house.

After the Maayaam ceremony comprising fun, frolic and joy, comes this ritual. Here, both the bride and the groom are asked to sit on a bed which is well decorated. They both are given the status of Lord Vishnu and Goddess Lakshmi at this moment. Parents of the groom along with several other relatives (married couples) present in the house, go around them, in a similar manner as was performed earlier by these two newly-weds. This ritual is called the *palangaachaar* or *palakaachaar* ceremony or circumambulating the bed.

This circumambulation around the newly weds sitting on the beds, is performed four times at some places, and seven times at others. After the completion of the last circumambulation, all the relatives present revere and honour both the newly weds by putting a vermilion mark with *kumkum* (*tilak*) on their foreheads, and present them gifts. These gifts usually contain silver or gold items. Sometimes cash is also given.

After this the royal priests bless the newly weds for a very bright and happy future. All the gods and goddesses of the family are worshipped and each one of them is revered by bowing heads in salutation before them and keeping a coconut, cash or gift before their idols. Besides this, on a small wooden stool, sweets, flowers, garlands, red coloured ritual thread, vermilion, turmeric powder, etc. are kept and both the bride and the groom circumambulate this stool seven times, beginning from the southern direction. This ceremony is called the *pher paataa* ceremony or going around the stool, signifying that the home of the bride has now changed.

After this, the *bidaaee* ceremony (departing of bride from the parents' house) is held.

Bride's Departure and Her Dowry (Vadhu kee Vidaaee and Daayajaa)

From the bride's side, presents, gifts, dowry items, etc. are given before her departure. Her hair is plaited and adorned. She is also asked to wear new clothes. This is usually done at the bridegroom's room at the wedding place. A precious metal head jewel (*teekaa*) is worn on her forehead. The groom's father is given gifts. All the present relatives are also given some coins and gifts. Women are seen singing ritual songs.

The newly-married couple are made to sit on a decorated bed for performing the *chaak* ceremony (worshipping the potters wheel). All her possessions and the items that are to be given as dowry are kept near this place. The relatives give presents and cash (*shagan*) to the bride after lifting her veil and seeing her face, perhaps for the last time after her marriage and departure for the new house of her groom. The ladies from the bride's side honour both the bride and the groom by putting a *tilak* (an ornamental mark on their forehead) and give some cash to them. The circumambulation of the bed on which both are sitting is made by the guests and married couples present there. The groom catches hold of the veil and *dupattaa* of both his parents-in-law and makes a demand for some thing. Till he gets a satisfactory reply from them, the groom does not leave the veil and *dupattaa*.

After all the rituals have been gone through successfully, the bride and her family are seen becoming sad and sentimental. The bride is soon going to be given farewell from her house. She ritually worships the entrance of the house. She is taken to the ritual place at the entrance and here the royal family priest makes her perform the ceremony with her own hands. At the entrance, the priest draws some sacred figures or diagrams. Some pieces of jaggery are kept on this drawing by the bride. Both her palms are filled with rice grains and sugar candies. She tosses them in the air behind her back.

Near the car, all the male relatives of the bride are waiting. They give her blessings and wish her good luck in her new life's beginning. Two or four attendants accompany the bride and take care of her.

The porchway in the bride's house is worshipped by both the bride and the groom before their departure. As per custom, the bride puts her hands' imprints of henna at the place. By tossing a handful of grains behind her back, the bride wishes for her parent's house peace and prosperity in her absence. It is departure time, and a new life for the newly weds. The women accompany the bride to her old living room. The whole atmosphere is very sombre and saddening. When the bride leaves her father's home (*baabul*), all the relatives join together and shower their choicest blessings on her. The bride is leaving behind all her family members, her relatives, and they will only be in her memories hence. Thinking about this repeatedly, she is saddened, confused, overwhelmed and heavy-hearted. The memories of her childhood days and friends haunt her. Fondness of her father, the soft and cushy lap of her mother where she could lie in comfort the whole day, attachment of her brothers, likings of her sisters, etc. will be the talk of the past now. When something most dear and precious is departing from someone, the eyes get automatically moistened. Tears flow down uncontrollably. The bride's tender heart bursts out with compassion and she starts weeping inconsolably. When the first line of the ritual song that is sung on the occasion is heard, all the ladies present join in the singing. Amid loud wails, hisses and sounds of weepings, they all console the bride and her mother. The whole atmosphere turns sombre, sad and heart-rending. There is not an eye left which has not been moistened here. Women are seen wiping their tears with the help of their veils. The sombre scene reaches its crescendo. All the relatives of the bride and their families — maternal uncles, paternal uncles, brothers-in-law, grandparents, etc. all join in. They embrace the bride — she, who had been their heart-throb till just a day earlier is today leaving all of them for her new home. They don't allow her to walk, instead she is seen being carried and hugged repeatedly with tears flowing from their eyes continuously. She is seen resisting and freeing herself from going further, and does not want to leave her father's place. But she is requested to go and is moved ahead slowly but steadily to the groom's side. The ritual songs are heard continuously. The words are heart broken amidst the wobbling, staggering and sombre voices.

थें घर जाओ दादा सा आपणे, बाई तो चाल्या परदेस,
संपत वे तो लावजो नीतर भला परदेस . . . ।

then ghar jaao daadaa saa aapne, baayee to chaalyaa parades, sampat ve to laavjo neetar bhalaa pardes. . . .

This moment is very touching. It almost splits the heart into two. The singing of ritual songs goes on hissingly and sobbingly. The father of the bride honours all the elder relatives from the groom's side and requests them with folded hands to take care of his precious daughter whom they had nurtured tenderly and with utmost care. And that she is very delicate and like a flower. They have loved and adored her all their lives. The bride's father also gives a suit or a shawl to his counterpart relative (groom's father or *samdhi*). The relative (*samdhi*) is requested to sit on a wooden stool. A silver bowl, filled with sugar, and with some cash kept on this bowl, is presented to him by the father of the bride. The bride's father pleads to forgive him if any work has not been performed up to their satisfaction. This ritual is also called the "sugar bowl" (*khaanda katoraa*) or giving money in a small box or chest (*peyi ke rupaye*). All the relatives of the groom are stamped with hand impressions of *roli* (red powder) and henna (*mehandi*) on their front and back sides. The relatives from the groom's side, on this occasion, usually seek donation from the bride's father in the form of a cow or cash for donating it to the guest-house where they had halted for the last few days to perform and solemnize this marriage ceremony.

At some places, the groom is even asked to kick the oven, while at some places he is asked to break the churning rope. This is an ancient ritual that is followed differently from place to place.

Farewell to the Groom Side (Samdhi Seekh)

At the time of the departure of the marriage group (*baaraat*), the groom along with his family members, relatives and friends is given farewell by the bride- groom's side relatives with songs and music band.

The bride's relatives are leading the procession followed by the groom and his relatives. At an auspicious place, usually a temple, the bride's father offers a coconut smeared with turmeric and some token cash and asks the groom's father to forgive him if anything has not been done as per his liking. The band master, a barber or any other attendant who have accompanied the *baaraat* (groom's procession) are given some cash, usually a lump sum amount. A coconut is placed near the front wheels of the vehicle accompanying the groom, water is poured on the wheels and worshipped. After this only the vehicle is signalled to move towards the groom's house.

The gifts that are given include ornaments, clothes and other household items. It is strictly kept in mind that no items made of iron like iron tongs, iron hot plate, steel lock, etc. are given as it is considered very inauspicious. Giving copper utensils is considered to be very auspicious. Besides these gifts, all relatives are also given gifts separately. Sweets are also given as a ritual which is later distributed in the whole village.

Welcoming the Groom along with his Bride (Var-Vadhu Vandan)

After the marriage ceremony is over, the marriage procession along with the bride departs. Information is given at the groom's place in advance about its arrival there.

The wedding procession prepares to go back, along with the bride, to its original destination from where it began its journey. The prior information is sent to the groom's place about its arrival. The barber is deputed to do this job and inform the arrival of the groom along with the bride first to the mother of the groom. Before they arrive, the house is thoroughly cleaned and decorated. New footsteps (signifying Goddess Lakshmi — the Goddess of Wealth) are printed at the entrance gate. Henna is put on the hands of all the ladies present in the house. On the arrival of the groom and the bride, all the ladies present converge at one particular place in the house, sing songs amidst the beating of drums. They accompany the groom and the bride inside the house on their arrival.

This ceremony usually takes place during the night, and the auspicious time is strictly followed. Nowadays, the bride and the groom reach home even during the day time. Earlier, the bride is asked to stay in a house of any neighbour for some time before reaching her own (in-law's) new house. She is treated here with equal respect and as one's own daughter or close relative only. For the bride, this is like her own father's house (paternal house or *peehar*) as long as she is staying with her in-laws. She is given a saree along with other gifts from this house.

Bride's Ceremonial Entry and her Divine Footsteps (Vadhu kaa Grih Pravesh and Pagaliyaa)

This ritual is about the first time entry of the bride and the groom into their new house after their marriage.

The mother of the groom stands at the entrance to welcome them. On their arrival, she does *aarati* to both of them. At the entrance, a glass containing the water of river Ganga (*gangaajal*) or a glass containing rice grains is earlier kept there. The bride, with her right toes lightly tilts the glass and spills the water or grains. In a large plate, a red solution made of *kumkum* powder (vermilion) is kept. She first keeps her right foot in this red liquid and makes an imprint on the floor while entering inside the house. These are the divine footsteps of the new bride considered to be the footsteps of Goddess Lakshmi Herself. It is ensured that the right foot of the bride steps inside the house first. This is considered extremely auspicious and is seen as the entry of Lakshmi Herself into the house. The bride's *lehangaa* (very wide skirt) is laced with silver and golden beads before her entry into the house.

The groom's sister and the paternal aunt perform the ritual of *baaranaa rukaaee* (stop them from entry). It is only after the groom gives cash or a gift to both of them that they give way for their entry. At the same time a lady spreads some leaves on their way up to the ritual place, probably making their path softer and greener.

After this, the ritual of picking the plates takes place. Seven plates containing *rotee* are kept in the courtyard on separate platforms or stools. The groom and the bride go near these plates. The groom touches each plate with his sword and the bride bows and picks up that plate. All the plates are lifted one by one and gathered at one place by the bride. She gives all these plates to her mother-in-law, bows and touches her feet. It is believed that if the plates do not make any noise, there will be no fights between the mother-in-law and the daughter-in-law. This ritual also signifies that the daughter-in-law should remain calm and quiet in the house and should be respectful to all.

The daughter-in-law is taken to the ritual place, where she bows her head. The mother-in-law sees the face of her daughter-in-law through the light of the lamp and gives her a ceremonial present. This is followed by rituals similar to those that took place earlier at the bride's house, and both the bride and the groom indulge in playing a game of gambling (*juaa-jui*); picking up cotton swabs from each other's body (*rooyee chunnaa*), untying the ritual thread (*kaankan doladaa*), etc.

On this very day comes the auspicious night which is considered very important, ritually. The rituals of *raatijogaa* (keeping awake the whole night) and *suhaagaraat* (wedding night) are performed. The bride and the groom are introduced to all the relatives present and blessings sought from each one of them separately. They are then taken to their room where they enjoy their first wedding night and start their new life with pleasure.

Bowing and Touching the Feet (Paggelagaai)

This ritual means bowing and touching the feet by the bride of each elderly woman from the groom's side.

Next day, immediately after the wedding night (*suhaagaraat*), early in the morning, the first thing that is done is to take bath and cleanse oneself and bow to the various gods and goddesses placed at the ritual *poojaa* (worship) room. Later the daughter-in-law (*vadhu*) bows and touches the feet of all the ladies present in the house and seeks their blessings. This ritual is called the *Paggelaagani* (touching the feet). The bride bows before each and every elderly woman, takes both her hands below their knees, touches their feet and rises only after the elderly lady has given blessings to her.

Sometimes it so happens that the bride does not leave some elderly women's feet unless they give her some ceremonial gifts or cash along with their blessings. These women are among the most important of this house.

Wedding Plate and Face Gazing (Suhaagathaal and Muhan Dikhaayi)

This ritual means that women on the groom's side look at their daughter-in-law's face for the first time after marriage.

The day after the wedding night, early in the morning, after getting fresh and worshipping the gods and goddesses, the ritual of untying the sacred threads (*kaankan doladaa*) is completed. This is immediately followed by the ritual of "face gazing," called the *suhaagathaal*. At some places the game of gambling (*juaa-jui*) is also played followed by the ritual of *kaankan doladaa* (untying threads) in exactly the same way as was performed by both the bride and the groom at the former's house a day earlier.

A large plate is brought. Some porridge or rice is put in this plate. The bride and the groom are seated together. They put into each other's mouth a morsel of food from the plate. Then the ladies of the house present some money and give morsels of food to the bride and groom. On this occasion only the ritual of seeing the bride's face takes place. In olden days, the ladies did not accompany the wedding procession to the bride's place. The reason was that the procession usually walked all the way down or was sometimes horse-ridden. Therefore, this ritual was performed by the ladies of the house, as they were very keen to have a look at the face of the newly-wed bride. Thus the ritual came into existence. The bride is usually asked to put a big veil on her head so that her face is covered completely. The ladies come one by one, lift the veil from the face and gaze very closely at the bride to their satisfaction. They give their heartiest blessings, besides cash or gift also to the bride. The senior ladies of the house, including the mother-in-law, elder sister-in-law, elder paternal aunt, etc. pray and wish for their new daughter-in-law's welfare and happiness and utter these words:

> दूधो नहाओ, पूतो फलो, कभी सिर भी मत दुखो,
> बीमारी दूर रहे, लक्ष्मी पास रहे, आए को आदर मिले,
> गए को नमस्कार . . . ।
>
> *doodo nahaao, pooto phalo, kabhee sir bhi mat dukho, beemaari door rahe, Lakshmi paas rahe, aaye ko aadar mile, gaye ko namaskaar. . .* ।
>
> *meaning*, may you bathe in liquid, be the mother of many sons, never face any problem, may illness desert you, may Lakshmi (wealth) remain always with you, welcome a guest with honour, when he leaves, give him a grand farewell. . ."

In this way, after the completion of this ritual of *suhaagathaal*, most of the ceremonies of the marriage have come to a close. The images of the various gods and goddesses earlier installed at the ritual place in the house, are taken down on an auspicious day to a river for immersion. All the guests are given an affectionate send-off and are repeatedly thanked for their attending the function. Before departing, some close relatives personally give blessings to both the bride and the groom and wish them a happy and prosperous life.

Other Programmes Connected with Marriage Ceremony

The hand-taking ceremony (*paanigrahan*) of royal houses includes various other rituals which are performed at different places. They are as follows.

Ritual of Prosperity (Haraabharaa kee Rasm)

After the ritual of cash offerings to the various gods-goddesses is over, the ceremony of wishing and praying for everyone's peace and prosperity is performed. In this ritual, sweets, dry fruits, etc. are sent to the groom's place of residence along with some green leafy vegetables, like coriander, mint or spinach leaves and *laddoo*s. There is also a custom of giving Rs. 4 as *milani* (a token for the customary embrace) by the bride's father to his counterpart (the groom's father).

Nowadays, instead of Rs. 4, four coins are kept with fruits and other items that are sent. The green vegetables that are sent along signify that the family should always remain fresh, happy and prosperous. The sweets are distributed amongst all neighbours signifying that the boy has been betrothed. From the boy's side, sweets, fruits, and gifts along with a *saari* for the bride are also sent as a ritual.

Call of a Respectable Lady (Suvaasini ko Bulaanaa)

Marriage rituals are performed with the help of daughter or sister, paternal aunt or niece from the house only. The presence of a sister and an aunt is very essential. A sister or a daughter who is present in her parents' house is called *suvaasini.* (She may be married or unmarried but must be staying with her parents.) The brother is sent to bring her to the marriage house. The brother accompanies his sister home, who is then wearing a new saree which was given by her brother, and the ceremonies begin. The aunt or sisters also bring along with them adornments and embellishments for the ceremony. The ritual ceremonies begin immediately. As the daughter arrives, the mother or sister-in-law of the bride or the groom takes the earthen pot along with other material she has brought inside and places it near the ritual place of worship.

The lady (aunt or sister) is taken near the place of worship and requested to sit on a wooden platform. The lady attendants of the house wash her feet with liquid and turmeric. After this, the lady is applied a *tilak* (a mark on the forehead). Sweets are given to her, and the women sing ritual songs. The sister brings along with her clothes and sweets for her brother. The sweets are later distributed amongst neighbours, sending a message about her arrival in the marriage house and that rituals for the marriage have begun. On that day, rice porridge is prepared.

Besmearing (T*eekaa)* (Pattaa Bharanaa)

This is a ritual of besmearing the forehead of the bride and groom. The first *teekaa* is done with *kumkum* (vermilion) and rice grains. After this, in the morning and evening *teekaa* is applied with gold dust, small tablets of gold or silver and pearls. During feasts heavy *teekaa*s are applied.

Displaying Plates of Jewellery, Gifts, etc.

This is the ritual of displaying the jewellery and gifts in large plates. During the time available after Ganeshji has been established at the ritual place and till the hand-taking ceremony is performed, four ladies accompanied by a small girl from the groom's side bring jewellery and clothes for the bride. One daughter-in-law who accompanies them spreads the cushion on which the bride sits. Another lady helps the bride wear the jewellery, while the third helps the bride spread a large towel on her lap, so that the gifts, cash, etc. are collected at one place only. The small girl who accompanies the ladies brings a plate of dry fruits and sweets for the bride and sweetens her mouth. The little girl is given some cash as a token of thanks.

The jewellery includes an ornament worn on the parting of hair (*maang*), round ornament for the forehead (*teekaa*), anklets with bells (*paayal*), etc. which are very essential. On this occasion, the bride's side gives cash and gifts to the attendants also. At some places plates containing dry fruits, etc. are given by the bride's side to all the persons comprising the groom's side. Sometimes, the items sent from the groom's side also include clothes for the bride, silver containers with some coins inside, etc. The bride wears this dress when she goes to her in-laws' and her grandparents-in-law's (*naani*) homes, where her *kholaa* (a loose end of her *saari*) is filled with lot of cash, sugar candies, dry fruits, etc. All this material is later distributed among the relatives, neighbours and friends. On this day, from the bride's house, about 50 kg of liquid and 11 kg of sugar are sent to the groom's house early in the morning. Nowadays this has been reduced to 11 kg of liquid and 5 kg of sugar only that are sent to the bride's in-laws' house. Bride's side also sends 21 kg of *laddoo*s (sweets) to the groom's house and 11 kg *laddoo*s to the grandparents-in-law's house. All this material is later distributed by the groom's side to the neighbours and relatives. Bride's grandparents also send 11 kg *laddoo*s to the groom's house.

After the grand feast (*jeeman*) betel leaves and nuts are served to all. The money that is given to the bride and the groom by the grandparents are accepted and later returned to them by adding some amount and putting vermilion mark on the cash.

When the groom also goes to his grandparents' house along with his bride, his *kholaa* (large bag) is filled with cash, dry fruits, sugar candies, etc. Here the groom introduces to his bride all his relatives — parents, aunts, uncles, cousins, etc. This ritual helps the bride to meet all of them and know about them closely.

Worshipping the Bride (Gharbaa/Gaur Poojan)

This ritual means worshipping the bride in the house or village, a site that is considered very auspicious. This *gaur* worship is an important ritual and has a special significance in our culture. The maternal aunt has the first right to perform this ritual, or else paternal aunt or sister-in-law can also perform it. Performing this worship by a brahmin or a poor girl is also considered auspicious and religious. People who perform the *gangaur* worship (a tree bearing pea-like fruits), perform this *poojaa* (worship) very religiously.

At the central place of worship (*poojaa chauk*), a small wooden stool is kept. The bride, wearing a new *saari*, preferably given by her maternal uncle, and decorated in fine jewelleries, is asked to sit on this stool. Near the ritual pillar, a pitcher is kept on which a lamp is lit. The bride's thumb is tied with a thread taken from a lotus stalk (*naal kaa dhaagaa*). The couple who is to perform the ceremony holds the thread, picks up the water pitcher, and goes round the pillar seven times simultaneously sprinkling the water while taking the rounds. The other people who are present also go round this pillar and follow behind the couple performing the ceremony. In some places, the people who go round this pillar are given some grains which they sprinkle on all sides while taking the rounds. In some other places, the bride also does the seven rounds dropping green gram (*moong*) all along the path. A circular plate with raised brim is kept with water, liquid and sacred *doorbaa* grass in it. The bride's feet are washed in this plate by the couple performing the ceremony. Then the bride is given cash, gifts, clothes, jewellery, etc. After this all the other relatives present give cash or jewellery to the girl. At some places, this *gaur* worship is performed immediately after the arrival of the *baaraat* procession.

Tying a Ritual Red Thread (Mauliyaa)

This ceremony is about tying a ritual thread of red

colour (*mauli*). The maternal uncle does the Ganesh Poojaa and ties the *mauli* on his nephew's right hand and then gives him new clothes, cash and gifts and his bag is filled with dry fruits, sugar candies, etc.

A turban is also tied on his head. The boy seeks blessings from all his elders and is given cash and gifts by all the relatives present.

Bride Visits a Brahmin's House (Brahman Bindaulaa)

The bride goes to a brahman's house and partakes the preparation made of *moong daal* (green pulses). Pulses and rice are earlier sent to the brahman's house. The brahman lady serves food, liquid and even gives a token of cash (*shagan*) and only then lets the bride go. Cash is also given to both the brahman and his wife. While returning from the brahman's house, the bride comes with a canopy over her head. The sister or the daughter of the house performs the *aarati* at the entrance on the bride's return.

Mark on Forehead (Teekaa)

In the case of marriage of the first child in a family, the mother receives gifts from her parents' house (*nanihaal*). In this ritual, a veil is put around her and Rs. 101 given to her. Her forehead is also anointed with a *teekaa* mark. The paternal grandmother is also honoured in this way. In special circumstances, this veil, instead of the boy's mother, is put on by her sister, and in case of a daughter's marriage, the daughter herself puts on this veil.

A Plait (Chotee)

On both the sides — the groom's and the bride's — there is a funny ritual of sending a *chotee* (a plait) for the father of the groom or the bride's father. The *maamee* (maternal aunt), on either side, brings this *chotee* for the groom's father or the bride's father, which she puts on his head, adorns him and then helps him wear a saree. This ritual has been revived due to its light moment of fun and frolic contained in it. It is celebrated only to enjoy and make the mood playful.

Gifts Giving Ceremony by Brother to Sister (Bhaat Bharanaa)

This is one of the important rituals in the Hindu tradition. *Bhaat* (boiled rice) is given by a brother and his family on the marriage of the children of his sister. At the appropriate time, both the brother and sister meet and perform this ritual. Nowadays, this ritual is held on the wedding day or on the previous day.

On this particular day, all the brothers and their families get together at their sister's house. The sister requests the elder brother and his wife (*bhaabhi*) to sit on the wooden stools kept in the centre of the ritual place. The sister puts *teekaa* with *kumkum* and rice grain on her brother's forehead, and gives him some sweets. The brother puts a veil around his sister. The sister gives cash, a coconut and dry fruits to her brother and his wife. The sister, after taking a *seenkh* (a split grass) over his brother's head, tosses it behind him. The sister's sister-in-law (husband's sister) offers sweet water to both the brother and sister-in-law, and for fun touches a drop on the brother's cheeks. The brother gives some money to the sister-in-law in return. Both the brother and the sister give money to their attendants. After this, all the brothers along with their families, starting from the elder to the younger, come and meet their sister/aunt. The sister embraces all of them individually and puts a *tilak* on their foreheads, offers sweets and coconut to them. Their children are also equally welcomed and given sweets after putting a mark (*tilak*) on their foreheads. The younger sisters and their children are also given cash and gifts. The lady attendant of the house washes the feet of the sister-in-law (*bhaabhi*) and gets some cash in return. After this, the brother gives to all gentlemen cash packets as *milani* and his wife gives the same to all the ladies present there. On this occasion, even the old and the aged uncles honour their sons-in-law by putting a *tilak* on their foreheads.

Worship at Marriage House (Biradh Morchaa)

On both sides — the groom's and the bride's houses — a day before the marriage date, the in-laws of the daughters of the house are invited for veneration. They all come in a group to take part in the ceremony. They are offered vermilion, sandal powder, flowers and sugar candies. After all of them have gathered, *aarati* is done to all of them together. Ritual songs are sung on the occasion. All the relatives are given coconuts, sugar candies and cash and are bidden farewell. The servants of the relatives are also given cash.

Groom's Anointment (Telvaan evam Nahachhu)

This ritual means, before the departure for the marriage ceremony, the groom is anointed by the ladies of the house with oil so that no evil eyes fall on him. The groom is taken to the ritual place in the house and anointed with oil by his mother, paternal aunt, sister, and sister-in-law. They all anoint the groom five to seven times from head to toe. *Shahnaaee* and drum music is played on this occassion. After this, his body is rubbed with the paste made of turmeric, gram pulses, perfumes, etc. This custom is known as the *telvaan* ritual. The attendants of the house clip the groom's nails on both his hands and toes. The whole atmosphere is livened up by music and ritual singing of songs called *Nahachhu geet*. This ceremony of *nahachhu* is not only celebrated in Rajasthan but also in Bihar and Bundelkhand. Goswami Tulasidaas has written a composition called *raamlalaa nahachhu* based on this ritual performed on Shri Raam before his marriage with Seetaa. On this occasion, women from the blacksmith community, betel leaf sellers, tailors, etc. bring gifts for the families where marriage is being performed.

The bride is also similarly anointed with oil and paste which is later rubbed on her whole body. Curd is also put on the head. But nowadays, due to presence of shampoos of various kinds, oil and curd are no longer in use. The bride's mother and elder sister observe fast on this day. The bride is asked to sit on the wooden stool near the ritual place. The married ladies perform the oil anointing ceremony of the bride from head to toe. They use both their hands and perform this ceremony seven times. At some places, even the bride's grandfather, father and father's elder brother also take part in this ceremony. The materials used in this ceremony include *roli* (sacred thread), henna, curd, besides oil and it is done very systematically starting from the feet, knees, hands, shoulders and head, doing it seven times. After completing this process, it is repeated similarly seven times in the reverse order. This ritual is called the oil anointing ceremony, or *tel chadhaanaa*.

After this ceremony follows the *jhola* ritual. In this ritual seven married ladies put curd on the heads of the bride and the groom. The bride's father helps in pouring water on the head while the mother massages it nicely. The mother touches the *roli* on the bride's forehead seven times. The bride puts some paste on the hands of seven girls. This paste is later used by these girls and rubbed on the body of the bride. Later this paste is rubbed off the bride's body by her sister-in-law or by the wife of the barber with a slightly tough hand. After this the bride goes to take bath. After bathing she stands on the wooden stool at the ritual place. Over her head a small crown (*chandev*) is placed and all ladies including the mother, sisters, and aunts put *tilak* on her forehead and perform *aarati*. They touch the bride with their veil four times. Her uncles and brothers give cash in her hand and help her to descend from the stool. The bride bows before a heap of pulses and rice grains. On her left hand and foot are tied the ritual thread, and bangles are put. Later the paternal aunt (*bhuaa*) and the bride break their fast after consuming some sweet bread and dine together with all relatives.

Knowing the Lineage of Bride and Groom's Family (Barnaa)

The people who are fasting on the bride's side, i.e. those who will give away the bride in marriage and the parents of the bride together perform this ritual by going to the groom's place. On reaching the groom's house, the priest first performs the worship of Lord Ganeshji and the sacred pitcher. The priest from both sides tell loudly the names of the great-grandfather, grandfather and father of the boy and the girl and their respective *gotras* (lineage) so that all those present will know the family names, and it is made known that both the boy and the girl *do not* belong to the same *gotra*. While the groom sits with a cloth tied around his head and face, his parents keep a gold coin in their hands and take a vow to accept the girl as *kanyaadaan*. This ritual is equally important like that of the hand-taking ceremony. The parents of the bride, considering the groom to be the incarnation of Lord Vishnu, symbolically wash his feet and worship him. They give him clothes, and a turban is tied on his head. His *kholaa* (large cloth bag) is filled with currency notes, coconut, fruits, cloves, and cardamom. Later, the mother of the bride anoints the groom from head to toe with the paste (*peethee*). The groom bows before the elderly relatives of the bride and extends his *kholaa* towards them. At some places this *barnaa* ritual takes place immediately after the ceremony of *milani* takes place on the arrival of *baaraat*.

Fun, Frolic Ritual — Laddoo Jhelaaee

This ceremony in marriage is basically performed for fun, frolic and enjoyment only. In this ritual, the groom is examined physically and mentally and his patience and temperament is tested. This ritual is performed in-between the time procession (*baaraat*) reaches the bride's place and the performance of *torana* ritual, i.e. some time during the *milani* ceremony. The bride's elder sister or her paternal aunt keeps with her a red cloth bag from which she tosses *laddoo*s one by one in the air and the groom has to grab the *laddoo*s with his right hand. It is seen how quick is the groom in catching the *laddoo*s and how many *laddoo*s could he grab. All the people enjoy this episode.

Tossing the *laddoo*s also means that in the same way as this sweet or *laddoo* is jumping with joy when tossed in the air, joy and happiness should rise within us and in our houses. The groom keeps the coin that is kept inside this red cloth bag and the remaining *laddoo*s are distributed among the processionists.

Exchange of Garlands (Varmaalaa)

Nowadays, after performing the *torana* ceremony, the bride and groom exchange garlands. This is called the *varmaalaa* ceremony. Flowers symbolize sweet smell, delicacy, beauty, grace, happiness and radiance. Flowers encourage us to be always happy and laughing. When all these are combined in a garland, a message of love is sent. In ancient days, the bride used to pick-up her own groom amongst the various contestants who were present in her *svayamvar*. Today this custom has taken a new form, and this is the first occasion when both the bride and groom meet, and they signify their acceptance of each other by exchanging garlands, or symbolically exchanging their souls, when they take the first step on their long journey called marriage by the Grace of God and with the blessings of all elders and well-wishers.

Nowadays, this ritual is performed on an elaborately decorated stage, and in a royal manner the bride and the groom are made to sit on huge throne-like sofa chairs. The bride sits on the right side of the groom. First the bride garlands the groom and then the groom puts the garland around the bride's neck. After this garland-offering, all relatives and friends of both the bride and groom go to the stage, congratulate the couple and give them presents in cash and kind. The photographers and the videographers are also seen clicking photos on this occasion. These photos and videographs are very useful in future and are kept as memorabilia. After this *varmaalaa* ceremony is over, the people from the bride's side invite their counterparts from the groom's side for a sumptuous dinner. The food is served to the groom's relatives with great care and love, and they are given cash token (*shagan*) also before they get up after having food.

But nowadays, most of the relatives from both

the bride's and groom's sides and friends join in and have food together thinking that the marriage functions are over. The ceremonies that follow after this, are attended by very few close relatives and friends from both sides.

Marriage Timings (Korath)

On the marriage day, a few elderly persons from the bride's side go to the grooms's side to request them that the wedding procession in the evening should reach their place in time only. (This is possible only when the groom's and the bride's houses are in the same town.) The groom is requested to sit on the stool. The priest conducts the *poojaa* ceremonies. The bride's father and other relatives put a *tilak* on the groom's forehead and give cash to his father. The bride's *maamaa* (maternal uncle) also gives cash to his counterpart, the groom's *maamaa*.

Narration of Couplets (Chhand)

After the circumambulation ceremony is over, both the groom and the bride are taken inside the bride's house to the ritual place. Here, the groom bows to all the gods and goddesses, whose images are present there. At some places, the groom does not bow before the gods and goddesses of the bride's side. Only the bride bows. The ritual is that after the bowing down ceremony is performed, the groom is asked to recite a couplet. After listening to the couplet, first the bride's mother, and followed by other ladies, give cash to the groom. The groom has to give all the cash to his brother-in-law (*jeejaaji*) because it is he who reminds the lines of couplets to the groom as it is the duty that is assigned to him only.

Lighter Moments of Marriage (Nandoi-Moosal Vivaah)

The marriage consists of rituals like circum-ambulations, various vows, bride-giving, putting *kumkum* in hair-parting and various other sacred rituals. After completion of all these programmes, on the next day, the preparation for breakfast for the groom begins which is called *kanwar kalevaa.*

At this time, the ladies from the bride's side are very particular about the hospitality extended to the groom and his relatives and guests. They regularly meet the groom's father, brother-in-law (*jeejaa*), *chaachaa* (uncle), and others and ask if everything was going fine and to their satisfaction. But at the same time they also pass light comments for the purpose of enjoyment only. They even sing songs, and depict the *moosal* (grinding rod) to be the bride to whom the *jeejaashri* can be married. All these jokes take place at the breakfast table only, where the groom's brother-in-law (*jeejaa*) is present and is heading the party.

The ladies enjoy this moment very much and many a time they deliberately put some small pebbles into the curry, or mix salt in water or mix some unwanted things in food and all this is done very deliberately. The ladies tell the witty and oversmart *jeejaaji* that the bride has been married to his *saalaa* (brother-in-law) so he can marry the *moosal*, if he wants to. They even tie one end of the veil to the *moosal* and the other end to the *jeejaaji*'s waist. They take out a fake wedding procession also. But all this in lighter vein, amidst fun and frolic only, and not meant to offend anybody.

Playing a Game of Dice (Chaupad Khelnaa)

Besides playing the game of *juaa-jui* (gambling), a game of *chaupad* is also very essential to test the skill of the bride and the groom (*chaupad* is a game like *chausar,* played with dice on a cloth or a board of cross-shaped layout). Thousands of years ago both these games were considered very essential. It required the expertise of a person, especially the males in the *Mahaabhaarata* too. After the game of *juaa-jui,* both the groom and the bride played this game of *chaupad* where winning- losing was a matter of fun and enjoyment only. This game judged the individual skill of both.

Royal Food Serving (Aasheervaad Samaaroh, Jimaai evam Brahman Banauraa)

After the completion of the wedding ceremonies, on the very next day, marriage feast of royal style is served. Here all near and dear relatives are invited. Nowadays this ritual has become less popular. It has been replaced by grand reception parties on the second day after marriage. Here the bride and the groom are seated on a stage tastefully and elaborately decorated. Very near to them, the stage for singers and musicians is erected. They sing marriage ritual songs. Many a time professional singers and dancers are also called for the occasion. Being photographed along with the bride and the groom has become very common nowadays.

People are served very delicious food which includes varieties of salads, fruit juices, icecreams, snacks, various varieties of sweets, breads, rice, curries of different types and purees, etc. Since the family gods and goddesses are being worshipped from the beginning of the marriage ritual, a large plate containing all varieties of food is taken and offered to the deities kept in the prayer room. This is done in the very beginning and it is only afterwards that the guests are allowed to consume food. The food varieties are all kept on the table and the guests are invited to have the same in the buffet style. It is "help yourself" system that avoids any complaint of bad service. After the food, the relatives are thanked for their attending the ceremony and a cover containing cash (or a token gift) is given to them by the groom's father while they leave the reception venue. This has become a new ritual nowadays. Normally, the parents of the bride and other elders from her house do not take any food at her in-laws' house. But, this restriction has seemingly eased now. At some places, the bride's parents and close relatives who accompany them to the reception party, first give cash and gifts to the groom's father and other relatives present as a gesture of good wishes and blessings, and only then consume any drinks or food. They believe that since it is their son-in-law's house, they should pay first and only then consume anything.

With the blessings of Lord Ganesh, the ceremony had begun. Therefore, as a ritual of thanksgiving to the Lord, five or seven or more brahmans are served food and given cash and gifts before they leave the place. This ritual is performed at several places even today.

The food consists of curry, thick bread cake (*baati*), etc. First a plate containing this food is taken to a Ganeshji temple and is offered to God as a gesture of thanks for his blessings and as a gesture of prayer for happiness and prosperity for all time to come. From there the food is brought back as *prasaad* and distributed. The Brahmans are then served food and cash and given gifts.

Blessings by the Maternal Uncle (Maamaa Saveraa)

In this ritual, the priest puts a *tilak* (ritual mark) on the forehead of the groom's *maamaa* (maternal uncle). After this, the uncle keeps something precious (say money, gold, etc.) in his hand and hides it under his thumb. He touches the tongue of the sacred lamp's flame seven times and takes it towards the bride and similarly repeats it seven times and takes it towards the groom's side. This is called the ritual of *maamaa saveraa.* It merely signifies uncle's (*maamaa*'s) blessings for the newly weds' happy married life.

Visiting a Temple (Devi Dhaam)

The day after the marriage functions come to a close, early in the morning after the bride takes bath, washes her head and getting refreshed, the bride and the groom are taken to the temple accompanied by the groom's relatives. They all bow their heads before the gods and goddesses. The bride and her two brothers-in-law (groom's younger brother (*devar*) and his *jeejaa* — sister's husband) strike each other with a small tender branch taken from a *neem* tree (a plant known for bitter fruits and medicinal qualities). They strike each other very lightly, seven times, as a ritual. As per custom nothing is eaten till the ceremony is completed.

Sister-in-law's Blessings (Gavaranaa-Gavarani)

After the marriage, this ritual is celebrated at the groom's house. Sixteen married women come to the groom's house and have lunch together with both the bride and the groom. The saree which the bride has brought from her parents' house, is given to her sister-in-law (*nanad* — husband's sister). The other ladies are marked with a *tilak* on their foreheads.

Bangles Examining by Mother-in-law (Coodaa Badaa Karnaa aur Laakh Lakheshar)

After the marriage ceremony is over, an auspicious day is selected. On this particular day, this ceremony is held. The bride takes out all her bangles and keeps them in her arms. The mother-in-law then puts a bangle made of red wax (*chooda*) at the front and back of the bunch of bangles on each hand and makes the bride wear them again. She gives some token money also to her new daughter-in-law.

Brother Visits His Sister (Pagapheraa)

After the marriage when the bride's brother comes to take her sister home from her in-laws' house he brings along some currency notes also as per ritual. He also brings a saree and a blouse for the mother-in-law along with baskets of fruits and sweets.

Henna is put on the bride's hands before she is given farewell from her in-law's house. Here, the married ladies sing ritual songs on the occasion.

When the bride reaches her home (*pagapheraa*) then the ritual of opening the canopy (*maandaa*) is performed. In this, seven small heaps of sweets (*halvaa*) are made. Some money is also kept on these heaps. This sweet (*halvaa*) is distributed amongst seven small girls. After this the *doladaa* (ritual red thread tied on the hand to protect from evil eyes) is opened and kept at some other place, or it is tied up for one and a quarter months. Afterwards this *dolaraa* is immersed in the running waters of the river. When for the first time the son-in-law (*jamaaee*) comes and has food at his in-law's house, the ladies present there sing ritual songs in praise of the *jamaaee* (son-in-law) and *jeejaa* (brother-in-law).

At the time of bidding them farewell, a veil is put around the daughter before she bows down at the entrance of her house. Ritually it is believed that as long as the daughter does not become pregnant, she is bidden farewell from her house by always putting something to fill her lap. A veil is also put around her. Nowadays, people give some gifts and also cash to the daughter which may include a *saari* for her mother-in-law, a shawl, etc. The daughter is also given saaries and items made of gold and silver, besides many other things.